The Case for
Commitment to
Teacher Growth

SUNY Series on Educational Leadership

Daniel L. Duke, Editor

The Case for

Commitment to Teacher Growth

Research on Teacher Evaluation

**Richard J. Stiggins
& Daniel L. Duke**

State University of New York Press

The research on which this work is based was supported in part by OERI under contract numbers 400-83-0004 and 400-86-0006.

Published by
State University of New York Press, Albany

For information, address State University of New York Press, State University Plaza, Albany, N.Y., 12246

Library of Congress Cataloging-in-Publication Data

Stiggins, Richard J.
   The Case for commitment to teacher growth.

   (SUNY series on educational leadership)
   Bibliography: p. 157
   Includes index.
   1. Teachers—United States—Rating of.
2. Teachers—In-service training—United States.
3. Career development—United States. I. Duke,
Daniel Linden. II. Title. III. Series: SUNY
series in educational leadership.
LB2838.S79 1988   371.1'44   87-12470
ISBN 0-88706-669-0
ISBN 0-88706-670-4 (pbk.)

10 9 8 7 6 5 4 3 2

Contents

List of Tables

Preface

Teacher evaluation is a key to school improvement. As we pursue excellence in education through the promotion of the professional development of teachers, we cannot overlook the potential contribution of the teacher evaluation process to that development. This contribution has been overlooked in the past. Very few teachers report experiencing any professional growth as a result of the lockstep, accountability-oriented evaluation procedures they have experienced.

Over the past three years, we have conducted a series of investigations designed to shed light on why evaluations have failed to improve teaching and how evaluation procedures might be changed to promote teacher growth and development. The results of that research are reported in this volume. Four studies are described in the order in which they were conducted, to share the evolution of our thinking on the revision of the evaluation process. The first step was a comprehensive review of the research literature on teacher evaluation. The second was an in-depth study of four district teacher evaluation systems. The third focused on the evaluation experiences of a few teachers who benefited from successful, growth-producing evaluations. And the final studies explored the ingredients and impact of the evaluation experiences of a large number of teachers.

As a result of these studies, we have devised a clear sense of the ingredients needed in evaluations to maximize the chances that teachers will grow professionally as a result of participating in those experiences. We have described those ingredients for practitioners in *Teacher Evaluation: Five Keys to Growth*, published jointly in 1986 by the American Association of School Administrations, the National Association of Elementary School Principals, the National Association of Secondary School Principals, and the National Education Association. The purpose of this volume is to report in detail the research underpinning that practitioner's guide.

We wish to express our appreciation to those who contributed to the completion of that research. First, thanks to Nancy J. Bridgeford for her scholarship and dedication in the completion of the first two studies, to Mildred Wait for showing us how to evaluate teachers in such a way as to help them grow, and to Jason Millman for his guidance in laying the foundation for the research. Thanks also to the faculty and staff of the following school districts for sharing their evaluation experiences: Battleground, WA; Centennial Schools (Gresham, OR); Evergreen Schools (Vancouver, WA); Dayton, OR; the island of Guam; North Clackamas Schools (Milwaukie, OR); Sherwood, Or; Silverton, OR; and Tigard, OR.

Further, we would like to express special appreciation to the following educators for taking the time and caring enough to share their experiences and insights with us in great depth: Richard Donan, Kenneth Krause, Moana Loa, Trudy Mishler, Wendall Myers, Gayden Schorling, Linda Simington, and Pat Smith.

Finally, we thank Sharon Lippert for her patience during careful preparation of the manuscript in all of its versions and forms.

Many have shared their wisdom. Our insights have passed through many eyes.

Richard J. Stiggins
Daniel L. Duke

ONE

Teacher Evaluation:
The State of the Art

The paradox of teacher evaluation is that it holds the potential to help nearly every teacher improve, yet in actual practice it helps almost no one. The potential of teacher evaluation
is no secret. Most states require regular evaluation as a matter
of law and justify the requirement, in part, on the basis of the
need for teachers to keep improving. Nearly all districts have
policies and/or collective bargaining agreements spelling out
evaluation procedures. Many of our most prominent reforms—
such as merit pay, career ladders, master teacher programs,
and the like—rest on the assumption that sound, effective evaluation procedures can be devised. In fact, however, the evaluations of teacher performance carried out in most schools are
brief, superficial, pro forma affairs involving a few moments of
classroom observation every year or two followed by the completion of a required evaluation report form, which is signed by all
interested parties and filed away never to be seen again (Wise,
Darling-Hammon, McLaughlin, & Bernstein, 1984; Stiggins &
Bridgeford, 1985). When this occurs, the terms of the collective
bargaining agreement and requirements of state law have been
met, yet literally nothing of value is achieved for teacher, student, school, or community. Such cursory assignments are in-
capable of serving the evaluation needs of schools interested in
rewarding outstanding performance (Popham, 1986) and do
little to promote the professional development of teachers (Stiggins & Bridgeford, 1985).

In fact, much of what has been conceptualized about teacher
evaluation over the past decade reflects this decidedly negative
perspective. In the literature review that follows, we will illus-

1

trate the dissatisfaction of teachers, the frustration of administrators, and the confusion of all parties as to proper purposes and methods of teacher evaluation. An examination of current evaluation practices and attitudes easily could lead one to a sense of futility regarding the improvement of teacher evaluation or its outcomes.

The purpose of this book, however, is to approach the teacher evaluation issue from a decidedly more positive perspective. We report the results of a series of four studies designed to uncover the problems inherent in current evaluation practices, find potential solutions to those problems, and identify strategies for implementing those solutions. This positive problem-solving approach to evaluation was spurred by our strongly held view that teacher evaluation practices should be defined in terms of the best possible outcome from an evaluation: the professional growth of the teacher evaluated.

Local teacher evaluation systems often are designed to serve two purposes. The first is a summative evaluation purpose, in which evaluation provides information for use in making personnel management decisions, such as dismissal, promotion, and salary increase. In this sense, evaluations provide accountability. The second purpose is to promote the professional development of teachers. In this case, evaluations provide information on teacher strengths and weaknesses, so appropriate training can be planned. Both purposes are important and can contribute to school improvement; but they are fundamentally different. They differ in terms of decisions to be made, interests served through evaluation, evaluation mechanisms, potential limitations and impact on teachers and schools. Those differences are spelled out in detail elsewhere (Stiggins, 1986).

Two differences bear directly on the reason for our focus on evaluation for teacher improvement. Those are the differences in the impact expected from the two kinds of evaluation on (a) overall school quality and (b) individual teacher growth. With respect to overall school quality, growth-oriented evaluation systems can affect more teachers:

> Accountability systems strive to affect school quality by protecting students from incompetent teachers. However, because nearly all teachers are at least minimally competent, the accountability system directly affects only a very few teachers who are not competent.

Thus, if our goal is to improve general school quality—and we use only those strategies that affect a few teachers—overall school improvement is likely to be a very slow process.

Growth-oriented systems, on the other hand, have the *potential* of affecting all teachers—not just those few who are having problems. There is no question that all teachers can improve some dimension(s) of their performance. (Stiggins, 1986, pp. 53–54)

In addition, if evaluation is to improve schools, it must encourage individual teachers to become better teachers. Accountability and growth-oriented systems differ in their management of this issue:

Accountability systems rely on (a) the requirement of law and contractual obligation to compel teachers to participate, and (b) the threat of personnel action to trigger growth when needed.

The effect of required participation is clear. If teachers are not doing the job, they must change or leave the profession. If they are doing the job, there is no impact. . . .

But a growth-oriented system must manage the motivation issue differently and therefore, its impact on the individual varies. Since it is neither legal nor feasible to *require* all teachers to demonstrate skills above the level of minimum competence, participation in growth systems cannot be required for competent teachers.

Teachers cannot be *obliged* to "attain excellence," however lofty such a goal might seem, because there is no universally acceptable definition of excellent performance. While standards of *minimum* competence can be defined and applied uniformly to all, the standards of defining excellence vary markedly from context to context and teacher to teacher. (Duke, 1985)

Motivation to participate in growth-oriented systems must come from within each teacher. For all teachers who can find that inner motivation, there is the promise of positive impact. (Stiggins, 1986, p. 54.)

We chose to focus our research on the development of better understanding of growth-oriented teacher evaluation, because we believe it offers the potential of much greater impact on schools. As a result, our research questions addressed the relationship between the evaluation process and teacher motivation to use the results to improve. By addressing the teacher evaluation process in this way, we felt we could promote a closer match between the potential of evaluation for contributing to school improvement and the actual contribution.

Given this philosophical orientation, we initiated the research with a review of professional literature on growth-oriented teacher evaluation processes.

Research on Teacher Evaluation*

The majority of school districts look to teacher evaluation as a means of improving teaching performance (Educational Research Service, 1978; Bolton, 1983). But given the ineffectiveness of current evaluation approaches, most are not achieving this goal to any impressive degree. To understand why, we explored four dimensions of teacher evaluation: the current context; characteristics of constructive, formative evaluation systems; research on the status of evaluation practices in schools; and the role—actual and potential—of evaluation in fostering teacher growth and development.

The Context of Teacher Evaluation

The current context of teacher evaluation is changing. Donald DuBois, former coordinator of staff development in Salem, Oregon, explains part of the impetus behind this change: "Teacher evaluation, historically, has been a mess. Teachers often feel naked and defenseless by the 'inspection' and 'report card' system. For principals, the teacher evaluation process is a gut wrenching, time consuming duty" (Lewis, 1982, p. 55).

Educational administrators are aware of problems with current evaluations. Responding to a national survey by the American Association of Secondary Administrators (Lewis, 1982), administrators specified the following needs:

- *Better definitions of effective teaching.* Although many evaluation programs attempt to define effective teaching,

---

*This section and the section that follows were originally published in Stiggins, R.J. and Bridgeford, N.J. Performance assessment for teacher development. *Educational Evaluation and Policy Analysis*, 7(1), 85-97. Copyright 1985, American Educational Research Association, Washington, D.C. Reprinted by permission.

most definitions center on teachers' behaviors—not on appropriately measured outcomes.

- *More trust in the process.* As one superintendent put it, "We need to know how to evaluate people and get them to feel good about it." In many places, the "spirit" of evaluation has been so structured by teacher contract agreements that it is almost "pro forma."
- *Proof of the link between evaluation and instructional improvement.* Until there is some specific indication that the process is worth the trouble, some say it will remain "pro forma."
- *More specifics on evaluation techniques.* Conferences, personal goal-setting, classroom observations—these are common approaches to evaluation, but administrators want to do them better.
- *More sensitivity to the needs of the evaluator, primarily the principal.* Many participants feel they have neither the skills nor the time for successful evaluations. Evaluators wonder what kind of training they should have and how they should be evaluated to be sure the system works. (p. 11)

As these comments show, administrators are often frustrated by current practices. Evaluation is time consuming, potentially disruptive to staff–administrator relationships, often distrusted and criticized by teachers, and seemingly ineffective in improving instruction.

Teachers also are critical of evaluation procedures. They often contend that assessment methods are inappropriate: the performance criteria by which they are judged are either unspecified or too general; classroom observations are infrequent and superficial; the factors evaluated often have little relationship to instruction; supervisory evaluations too often are subjective, based more on personal characteristics than instructional skill; and results either are not communicated or are not useful in improving performance (Natriello & Dornbusch, 1980–81; Borich & Fenton 1977; Bolton, 1973).

Recent surveys of teachers' attitudes about evaluation bring these problems into sharper focus. For example, Wood and Pohland (1979) report that only 28 percent of the items in school districts' evaluation checklists relate to the instructional role of the teacher. A few additional items deal with such relevant personal characteristics as responsibility and enthusiasm. But the remaining checklist items relate to behavior outside the classroom: memberships in organizations, and participation in professional, social, and administrative activities. In other words, the criteria used in these instruments, note Wood and Pohland, appear unrelated to improving teaching performance and offer little assistance in changing teaching practices.

In studies conducted by Natriello and Dornbusch (1980–81), teachers noted that they viewed their evaluation systems as generally unsound, overly subjective, and unaffected by their efforts. Teachers in these studies indicated that evaluation criteria were seldom shared with teachers, that teachers were uninformed about the information collected to evaluate their performance, and that minimal time was taken to communicate evaluation results to them. The authors note, "The teachers in our interview study reported that on the average they received formal evaluations from their principals once every three years." Moreover, in these teachers' perspectives, evaluations were unrelated to the sanctions or rewards of the system and hence "had little value" (p. 3).

Levin (1979), in a summary of research on teacher evaluation, argues that "research provides little support for current practices in teacher evaluation." He goes on to comment, "One of the few things that can be safely said is that the prevalent system of evaluation . . . through observation by supervisors is biased and subjective. The use of techniques that have greater promise for providing objective data, such as observation instruments . . . is as yet uncommon" (p. 244).

Designing a More Constructive Environment

Dissatisfaction with current evaluation procedures and outcomes has prompted many educators to propose substantive revisions—revisions in planning, in designing performance criteria and acquiring meaningful data, and in communicating results to teachers. The following suggestions represent a concise cross section of current thought on what strategies might make evaluation practices more constructive and effective.

Manatt (1982), a major proponent of an evaluation model being tried in school districts across the country, advocates an evaluation system manifesting these features: (a) teacher involvement in the evaluation process; (b) centralized and collaborative development of performance criteria based on research and on local priorities; (c) goal setting; (d) multidimensional methods for assessing teachers' skills, including objective data gathering and self and peer evaluation; (e) analysis of results with teachers and development of specific job targets for improvement; and (f) inclusion of a preobservation conference to acquire background data and a postobservation conference to mutually analyze classroom data and set goals for improvement.

Manatt's model strongly reflects the positive impact of clinical supervision, a collegial process of professional development designed by Harvard School of Education faculty in the 1960s. Clinical supervision is a system in which teacher and supervisor work together to set goals and determine progress. This collaborative model includes three major steps: preobservation conferences to exchange background information and to mutually establish goals and methods for gathering data; multiple classroom observations that include collection of objective data; and post-observation conferences to analyze and verify data and to collaboratively develop a systematic plan for improvement. In addition, the teacher and supervisor communicate extensively throughout the evaluation process to ensure that the teacher has a real voice in determining evaluation procedures and setting goals for professional growth. Although clinical supervision methods have been adopted procedurally by districts across the country, the heart of the teacher development process—frequent observation and discussion—has not been successfully incorporated into most local systems.

In response to valid concerns about the perfunctory nature of most evaluations and reliance on subjective observational data, many educators urge the use of (a) assessment methods that give more adequate and objective data about classroom interactions (verbatim records, charts of classroom interactions, records of questioning, or reinforcement strategies); and (b) use of multiple evaluation procedures (student and peer evaluation, assessment of student products) to provide a more comprehensive picture of the teacher's performance (O'Hanlon & Mortensen, 1977). Levin (1979) reinforces the need for "more extensive use of student evaluations and less reliance on ratings by principals and other supervisors" (p. 244). He also concludes that "reliance on a single evaluation technique is unwise" since it reduces the possibility that the teacher will be judged fairly.

Following a comprehensive analysis of current teacher evaluation practices, Darling-Hammond, Wise, and Pease (1983) specify four minimal conditions for a successful teacher evaluation system:

- All individuals in the system understand the criteria and processes for teacher evaluation;
- All participants understand how these criteria and processes relate to the basic goals of the organization; i.e., there is a shared sense that the criteria reflect the most important aspects of teaching, that the evaluation system is consonant with their educational goals and conceptions of teaching;
- Teachers perceive that the evaluation procedure enables and motivates them to improve their performance; and principals perceive that it enables them to provide instructional leadership; (p. 320)
- All individuals in the evaluation perceive that the evaluation procedure allows them to strike a balance "between adaptation and adaptability, between stability to handle present demands and flexibility to handle unanticipated demands" (Weick, 1982, p. 674). That is, it allows participants to achieve a balance between control and autonomy.

Achieving a More Constructive Environment

How extensively do current school practices incorporate these commonly advocated criteria? In summarizing a series of surveys of evaluation practices, Knapp (1982) contends that despite strong advocacy of multiple information sources, involvement of students and peers, and more objective means of collecting data, schools have not really changed their approach to teacher evaluation. Principals still do most of the observing; staff members are seldom involved in planning; and little real effort is made to use evaluation outcomes in designing constructive staff development.

Similarly, a recent analysis of thirty-two highly developed current teacher evaluation systems across the country, completed by the Rand Corporation under sponsorship of the National Institute of Education, provides these insights regarding evaluation practices (McLaughlin, 1982):

Exemplary programs displayed a number of common features. Nearly all of the thirty-two programs studied required a preevaluation conference (88 percent), classroom observation (100 percent), postevaluation conference (100 percent), a written action plan following evaluation (88 percent), follow up of the action plan (81 percent), and the participating principal as primary evaluator (78 percent). Few, however, used self-evaluation (38 percent), peer evaluation (25 percent), or students' achievement data (22 percent) in evaluating teachers.

Despite these similarities, McLaughlin (1982) suggests "there is scant agreement about instrumentation, frequency of evaluation, role of the teacher in the process, or how the information could or should inform other district activities" (p. 11). In other words, little consensus exists about "best practice." Moreover, although 74 percent of the districts named school improvement or staff development as the primary goal of the system, few districts established the necessary links between teacher evaluation and staff development to make that goal achievable. There is, as the study notes, "a general lack of integration between teacher evaluation and staff development or district curriculum guides" (p. 11). Thus, although exemplary programs appear to emphasize staff development and school improvement, more often than not, teacher evaluation operates as an independent, self-contained system, not an integral component of a broader staff development program.

As Knapp (1982) notes, strong formative evaluation programs required both staff involvement and a speciied relationship between teacher development and evaluation. But despite the urgings of researchers and educators themselves, not much has happened. Knapp states, although effective evaluation of individual teachers can provide "a more accurate picture of an individual teacher's needs than, for example, the group needs assessments commonly used . . . systematic evaluation of individual teachers does not as yet appear to be a standard part of staff development planning" (p. 8).

Holley (1982) contends that districts need to make better use of evaluation data. "When evaluator ratings are summarized across competencies or areas, the training needs of both evaluatees and evaluators emerge" (p. 7). District and building summaries can be instrumental in identifying staff development needs. "The data," argues Holley, "should be captured and used for the improvement of both the evaluation process and instruction" (p. 7).

While teacher evaluation practices are becoming more systematic procedurally, most are still insufficient to support viable teacher improvement programs. At the very least, teachers want an evaluation system that provides accurate information on classroom needs, opportunity to acquire and master new learning approaches, and collegial support when instigating needed changes. These activities demand more time, more instructional involvement, and more thorough assessment than many principals seem to find manageable. As a consequence, practices become more formalized, remaining basically unchanged. Moreover, as the next section indicates, changes in practice may occur more in response to external pressures than to internal needs.

Factors Regulating Teacher Evaluation Practice

State teacher evaluation laws and regulations can influence local evaluation practices, as can collective bargaining agreements. This section explores whether these laws and contracts promote or constrain the use of evaluation for teacher development.

We begin our analysis of state laws and regulations with a brief summary of the national picture, then comment on district–teacher association contracts.

Teacher Evaluation Laws

According to Wuhs and Manatt (1983), twenty-six states had laws requiring teacher evaluation in that year. The number of such laws had increased dramatically during the prior twelve years, with over 80 percent of all laws enacted since 1971. That rate of increase has continued, with thirty-six states requiring teacher evaluations in 1985 (NEA, 1985).

Wuhs and Manatt report that in nearly all states, improvement is a primary purpose; in almost half, evaluation data are also used for personnel purposes. Beckham (1981), by contrast, reports that less than half of the states list school or teacher improvement as their primary purpose, and that the remainder of laws serve personnel decision-making functions. This apparent discrepancy may indicate simply that most evaluation laws serve multiple purposes and often claim to address both formative and summative issues.

Three quarters of the states leave control of evaluation procedures to local districts. Very few specify criteria to be evaluated. And still fewer provide any guidelines for the development of local systems. So it is apparently local decisions, not state mandates, that determine most district evaluation procedures. Since local procedures are often negotiated as part of collective bargaining agreements, state laws, as a general rule, would appear to have minimal influence on promoting or limiting any local emphasis on formative teacher evaluation. However, they may indirectly impede formative practices by requiring certain procedures, such as use of uniform, mandated evaluation reports or rigid specification of teaching criteria unrelated to district identified teaching priorities. In such instances, evaluators may first meet the formal, state-mandated requirements and then may decide that implementation of added formative practices is not (a) necessary or (b) possible, given other time demands.

Although some state laws do include provision for teacher development, most are far less prescriptive than the law passed in Connecticut for the purpose of mandating formative evaluation. The Connecticut State Department of Education (1979) specifies the following evaluation methods:

- Cooperative planning between professionals and evaluators of the objectives of each individual evaluation, the evaluation procedures, and the process of evaluating the system by staff,
- Clear specification and communication of the evaluation purposes as well as the specific responsibilities and tasks that will serve as the frame of reference for individual evaluations,
- Opportunity for teachers to evaluate themselves in positive and constructive ways, and
- Emphasis on diagnostic rather than evaluative assessment with specific attention given to analyzing difficulties, plan-

ning improvements and providing clear, personalized, constructive feedback.

As our discussion will show, these state guidelines attempt to establish a stronger tie between teacher evaluation and teacher development than do most.

The Impact of Collective Bargaining Agreements

A major force in defining and limiting district teacher evaluation procedures has been the collective bargaining agreement. Its chief impact has been to provide due process safeguards for teachers. According to Strike and Bull (1981), who studied numerous such agreements, these contracts affect the evaluation process by specifying the frequency of evaluations or observations, informing teachers of evaluation criteria, restricting some methods of information gathering (e.g., unannounced visits, secret monitoring, electronic equipment, etc.), and specifying who can and cannot participate in the evaluation process. They also often require formal communication of evaluation results, regulate written reports (e.g., confidentiality, opportunity for a written response by teachers), require remediation for negative evaluations, allow union representation at all conferences and procedures, and necessitate that notice and reasons be filed for disciplinary action, dismissal, or demotion.

The effect of these contracted agreements is to promote uniformity and specificity in evaluation procedures. Because of the adversarial nature of many contract negotiations, teacher evaluation also is becoming more rule governed and focused on clearly specified minimum work standards (Mitchell & Kerchner, 1983). Collective bargaining seemingly has done little to promote links between teacher evaluation and individual development. Although it has often clarified evaluation requirements, it also has had the effect of making evaluation procedures more impersonal and unintentionally introduced a dimension of divisiveness into the evaluation process.

The legal and contractual factors governing teacher evaluation typically are designed to standardize evaluation requirements and to promote due process in summative evaluation. By promoting adherence to fair practices in personnel decision making, however, in effect, they have directed attention toward legal requirements and away from methods for promoting teacher growth and development. Although it is encouraging to find some state laws attempting to strike a balance between formative and summative teacher evaluation, the laws only set an overall context for practice in districts and schools. Their effectiveness still depends on interpretation and implementation. Regulations indeed may enhance the potential for improvement, or they may be viewed as just one more requirement to be met, thus having little substantive impact on instructional changes.

The Research Sequence

In the chapters that follow, we describe a sequence of three additional studies arising from the foregoing review and exploring teacher evaluation in its current state (as just described). In conducting these studies, we sought to understand how the evaluation process could be changed to promote teacher growth. The description that follows is designed to communicate the evolution of our thinking about the evaluation process over a three-year period. Each study and its implications are written to communicate our perspectives at the time the study was done, without knowledge of the results of subsequent studies. We felt it important to reflect the evolution of our thought because the time sequence reveals how each study follows from and reinforces the results of the studies that preceded it. The total effect is to add strength to our conclusions about effective teacher evaluation practice drawn in the final chapter.

The first step in our inquiry into teacher evaluation practice was to discover first hand how existing laws and collective bargaining agreements were translated into actual district practice. This step involved the completion of case studies of four local evaluation systems. The results of those studies are reported in Chapter two. The initial questions were these: Do local evaluation concerns mirror those identified by other researchers? What is the intended relationship between teacher evaluation and teacher growth? What is the actual relationship? If, as expected, evaluation fails to promote teacher improvement, why does it fail? What are the barriers to a closer link between teacher evaluation and improvement? We succeeded in obtaining answers to these questions in Study 1.

Although the first study suggested needed changes, political and practical realities made it virtually impossible to conduct a validity study to test the impact of change within a functioning school district. For this reason, we devised a study, described in Chapters Three and Four, in which we identified instances of successful teacher evaluation and explored the antecedents to success. We defined success as an evaluation that actually resulted in teacher improvement. Thirty teachers who had experienced growth through effective evaluation were interviewed, the evaluations profiled, and the profiles compared. The comparison revealed that evaluation involving certain types of teacher evaluators, data collection procedures, feedback, and context of the evaluation have a high probability of helping teachers grow. In Chapters Three and Four, we describe those attributes and illustrate their importance with actual teacher interviews.

Having explored a limited number of successful evaluations, we were able to assemble a comprehensive questionnaire in which any teacher could rate the important attributes of his or her last evaluation. In Chapter Five, we describe the results of the administration of that questionnaire to 450 teachers in five school districts. Responses to the fifty-five-item instrument were analyzed in such a manner as to profile the typical evaluation within and across districts, explore variation in evaluations, and probe the relationship between attributes of an evaluation and its overall quality and impact on the teacher. This chapter reports the results of these analyses in detail, showing how they validate the results of the previous studies and reveal the highest priority attributes of a growth-producing evaluation event. The results also reveal the value of the questionnaire for probing needed changes in any local teacher evaluation system.

The sixth and seventh chapters assess the implications of the research program for the future of teacher evaluation research, policy, and practice. Models are presented for designing evaluation systems that rely on cooperation and trust to promote school improvement. Research questions that remain unanswered are disucssed as we tie the three studies together and look to the future.

TWO

Case Studies of District Teacher Evaluation Systems

The goal of the first study* was to gain detailed knowledge of the nature of the teacher evaluation environment and the management of teacher improvement issues within that environment. To reach this goal, we examined the teacher evaluation systems of four Pacific Northwest school districts. The districts were recruited to participate in the research on a voluntary basis. Two were located in the state of Washington and two were in Oregon. Of the two Washington districts, one was suburban (enrollment of 13,200 with two high schools, four middle schools, and thirteen elementary schools) and the other was in a community about 30 miles from a metropolitan area (enrollment of 7100 with two high schools, four middle schools, and five elementary schools). Both Oregon districts were suburban. One enrolled 6800 students with one high school, two middle schools, and nine elementary schools. The other reports attendance of 11,500 in three high schools, four junior highs, and eighteen elementary schools.

The case studies were completed according to procedures described below and district teams were brought together to hear, discuss, compare, and interpret the results. Both the case

---

*The case study descriptions and results were originally published in Stiggins, R. J. and Bridgeford, N.J. Performance assessment for teacher devleopment. *Educational Evaluation and Policy Analysis,* 7(1), 85-97. Copyright 1985, American Educational Research Association, Washington, D.C. Reprinted by permission.

study results and outcomes of the interpretive conference are described in this chapter.

Case Study Methodology

To learn about teacher evaluation practices in these districts, two researchers conducted interviews with district administrators in charge of teacher evaluation and with building principals (elementary, junior high, and high school). In addition, each principal was asked to name four teachers from her or his school who could be interviewed or respond to a questionnaire on teacher evaluation practices.

All participants were asked to describe teacher evaluation practices from their viewpoint. Further, they were asked if and how they used results to plan teacher development. Interviews and questionnaires touched on state and district policies, development of evaluation procedures, methods for gathering information on teacher performance, methods for communicating evaluation results to teachers, and relative satisfaction with the evaluation system. In outlining ways evaluation data are used, administrators and principals described the specific decisions influenced by the results. They also were asked what role teacher evaluation plays in promoting teacher growth and improvement. Results of the interviews and questionnaires are summarized in Table 1.

Case Study Results

In summarizing case study results, we found evaluation procedures to be strikingly similar across districts. Results are presented in detail in Table 1. For example, all districts used a three-stage evaluation process including a pre- and postobservation conference and classroom observation. The observations, conducted either by principals or vice principals, were the central feature of all evaluations. They occurred formally either once or twice a year. Peers and students were seldom involved in the evaluation; self-evaluations were cursory if done at all, and student achievement data did not play a role in evaluation. Results of the evaluator's observation were communicated both in person and in writing to the teacher. The written reports called for supervisors to describe teachers' strengths and weaknesses on either state or locally specified criteria. None of the districts used rating scales or indications of performance levels to identify teachers' skills. Finally, training provided evaluators ranged from a frequent, integrated program that involved all staff, in one district, to intermittent or sporadic training in other districts. In addition, both teachers and administrators saw room for improvement in the evaluation process and made specific recommendations about needed changes.

Teachers' Perspectives on Needed Changes

The primary goal of our case studies was to identify barriers inhibiting use of teacher evaluation results for teacher growth and development. In this regard, teachers were asked for their perspectives on

* Changes needed in the teacher's role in evaluation,
* Changes needed in district procedures, and
* Ideas for improving the quality of teaching in the district.

With respect to the teacher's role, over half (53 percent) spontaneously urged more opportunity for collegial observation and for self-evaluation through goal setting and videotaping. Others suggested providing teachers more information about what constitutes effective teaching and more proficiency in evaluating lessons.

Recommendations for improvements in the overall evaluation system were far more extensive. Repeatedly, teachers suggested more frequent formal and informal observations, greater use of peer observation and self-evaluation, and more effective preparation and training for evaluators. In addition, they called for better observational strategies, more effective communication of results, with emphasis on specific suggestions for improvement, increased skill among evaluators, and better general management of evaluation. Teachers also noted that they needed high-quality in-service training to improve their skills.

Teachers tended to feel that to be effective, evaluation must (a) be a valued schoolwide high priority, not just a requirement; (b) occur frequently enough so that outcomes reflect actual classroom activities; (c) incorporate methods that provide rel-

TABLE 1
Teacher Evaluation Summary

Evaluation Component	District 1	District 2	District 3	District 4
1. Frequency of Evaluation	Tenured: 2 observations per year Nontenured: 2 observations per year	Minimum of 3 visits year Probationary: 4 visits	Tenured: 2 visits Probationary: minimum 3 visits	Tenured: 1 visit per year Probationary: 2 visits per year
2. Impact of Collective Bargaining Agreement	Contract is precise and prescriptive	Sets up formal structure	Set some procedures Does not constrain	Sets some procedures Does not create restraints
3. Instrument Used Evaluation Categories/ Criteria	Prescribed by state law: 1. Professional preparation and scholarship 2. Knowledge of subject matter 3. Instructional skill 4. Classroom management 5. Handling of disruptive problems 6. Interest in teaching pupils 7. Effort toward improvement when needed	Prescribed by state law: 1. Professional preparation and scholarship 2. Knowledge of subject matter 3. Instructional skill 4. Classroom management 5. Handling of disruptive problems 6. Interest in teaching pupils 7. Effort toward improvement when needed	1. Diagnosing needs and abilities 2. Prescribing (learning activity) 3. Facilitating activities to accomplish outcomes 4. Evaluating growth and development 5. Student relationships and classroom management 6. Professional relationships	1. Diagnosing 2. Teaching: teach to objective, monitor progress, revise and adjust lesson 3. Managing: classroom atmosphere, evaluate and document student progress 4. Responsibility as professional 5. Responsibility to parents and community 6. Responsibility to school district
Nature of Form	Narrative; asks for description of strengths, weaknesses, suggestions for improvement. No scaling or rating Inadequate space for detailed commentary Subjective rating Teacher's signature required	Narrative called for; form provides room for minimal comment Teacher's signature required	Form does not address each area. Has 3 major questions: e.g., In what ways has teacher met, failed to meet, or exceeded performance standards? No rating, all narrative Teacher's signature required	Form does not address each area. Has 3 major questions: e.g., In what ways has teacher met, failed to meet, or exceeded performance standards? No rating, all narrative Teacher's signature required

4. Administrators' Perspective on Role of State Law	Specify clear procedures and timelines for due process / Without guideline, probably would not get done—time issues	Gives kick to do evaluation / Procedurally, no help at all	Has specified form; restricts but does not handicap / Can do good job within system	Has minimum standards / District requires more than the law
5. Evaluation Stages	Preconference / Observation / Postconference	Preconference / (No formal goal setting) / Observation / Postconference	Written: individual, building, district / Preobservation / Goal setting / Observation / Postobservation	Target: written, submitted / Preconference (form) / Observation / Postconference / Plan if needed
6. Who Evaluates?	Principal, assistant principal	Principal or department heads	Principal and other building administrators	Principal / Department heads and part-time evaluator
7. How and When Was System Developed?	Developed via contract bargaining; last major changes in 1979	Process of negotiation with teachers / Administrative group studied and planned system	Developed in 1979–80 for 1980–81 by committee of teachers and administrators	Committee of teachers and administrators, through steering committee of mostly teachers
8. Role of Other Evaluation Sources	(None specified by district)	(None specified by district)	(None specified by district)	(None specified by district)
Peer	No role	No role	No role	No role
Student	No role	Used independently by some teachers	No role	One principal has students evaluate courses
Self-Evaluation	One principal used questionnaire to analyze lesson (for teacher)	Informal self-evaluation	Used informally, through questioning strategies	Informally, through analysis of lesson
Student Achievement	No role	No role	No role	No role
9. Training Provided in Evaluation	Appears to be individual training / Systematic district training seems minimal	Some district training; principal and administration view on amount and emphasis differs	District workshops provided regularly	Strong training program / Teachers trained in ITIP, ITIP focus of instruction
10. Formal Relationship to Staff Development Training	School: use informally / District: evaluation not well enough written to identify needs	School: informally / District: no direct link to staff development planning	School: some use informally, others rely on administration and department heads to select training / District: not used	School: not done formally / District: not formally, but staff development is viewed as influencing evaluation process, determines form of evaluation

evant, specific, complete information; and (d) involve evaluators trained to provide specific, useful suggestions for improvement. Repeatedly, teachers called for more frequent feedback and for constructive criticism, not "vague generalities that hide mediocre teaching."

Administrators' Perspectives on Needed Changes

How satisfied were building principals and district administrators with their evaluation systems? Responses differed considerably across districts.

In two districts, administrators were generally satisfied with the evaluation process, but concerned with the amount of time available to conduct observations. In the two other case study districts, administrators were less satisfied. Reasons for dissatisfaction included teachers' lack of trust in the evaluation process, lack of clarity in criteria, and the fact that evaluation seemed more oriented to meeting state standards than promoting improvements.

Similarly, not all agreed that teacher evaluation led to teacher improvement. Some felt that the goal-setting process was a major step toward improvement and that, increasingly, evaluation was focusing more on improvement than on judgment. Others felt the link was weak at best. Principals also generally acknowledged that evaluation results were not directly used to plan school or districtwide staff development and that local supervisors did not include evaluation results in setting instructional priorities. However, evaluation was used by some evaluators to help teachers identify individual goals and to specify a plan of action for the year. The completion of these plans and their effect on instruction were seldom monitored.

Administrators cited four major barriers limiting the development of a more formative evaluation system: (a) teachers' lack of trust in the process; (b) insufficient time for evaluation; (c) the adversarial context of evaluation; and (d) the principals' skills as evaluators. The trust and time were issues mentioned by nearly every administrator interviewed. Principals also noted these problems: inconsistent evaluation procedures, imprecise requirements, lack of training for evaluators, imprecise dismissal procedures, overly general evaluation outcomes, teachers' resistance to change, and inadequate staff development. Administrators noted, too, that many principals did not know how to establish evaluation programs or set realistic priorities.

When asked how evaluation could be related more directly to the improvement of teaching, administrators recommended changes in system management, including increased staff involvement in goal setting and emphasis on improvement as a district priority, improved methods of conducting observations, more time allowed for evaluation and observations, development of evaluators' skills, a stronger link between evaluation and staff development, and accountability for all principals conducting evaluations.

In summary, supervisors say that evaluation can be more effective in diagnosing teachers' needs and improving their skills, but only if the process changes in many ways. And, the major changes they recommend closely parallel the concerns identified in national studies of teacher evaluation.

A Conference on Teacher Evaluation

At the conclusion to the district case studies, teams of educators—each team including a district administrator, a principal, and a teacher from each of the four case study districts—were invited to attend a working conference to consider, in greater depth, methods for more effectively linking evaluation and staff development within the districts. Conference teams discussed two major issues: the barriers to growth through teacher evaluation; and potential ways of more closely linking evaluation to teacher improvement.

After reviewing the results of the case studies of their districts, conference participants worked together to produce a common list of barriers to formative teacher evaluation (listed in order of importance):

1. Evaluators often lack important skills needed to evaluate teachers, and the training needed to solve this problem is frequently not available, not used, or ineffective. At least two sets of skills are lacking: skills in evaluating teacher performance; and skills in communicating with teachers about the evaluation process and results.

2. There is often insufficient time for both evaluation and follow up. A continuous cycle of feedback and growth is needed to promote teacher development. The competing demands of education frequently reduce evaluation to a low-priority status.

3. The process for linking staff development and teacher evaluation is not clear. Schools lack a clear goal for formative teacher evaluation (i.e., an image of the desired system) and a plan for achieving that goal. State laws and district policies and procedures do not reflect that goal; and individuals within the system (teachers and administrators alike) have yet to provide the support needed to make evaluation results truly productive. While an important emphasis is placed on protecting the due process rights of teachers, evaluation systems lack a similar commitment to promoting professional development.

4. Trust in the evaluation system often is lacking among educators functioning within that system. Unclear or unacceptable performance criteria combined with lack of teacher involvement in developing performance criteria and infrequent and superficial observations, tend to breed skepticism among teachers about the value of results. The adversarial relationship between districts and collective bargaining units also may contribute to distrust.

Having identified a list of significant barriers, conference participants then turned to the task of finding solutions. They noted that commitment to effective teacher evaluation as an important means to school improvement must be given a high priority within the district. School districts need to determine the foremost purpose of their evaluation, either staff improvement or personnel decision making, and develop procedures appropriate to that purpose. Added to these initial steps, conference participants called for

- Involvement of all staff members in the planning process,
- Identification of meaningful and relevant performance criteria as the basis of the evaluation,
- Evaluators trained to pinpoint teachers' skills in need of development,
- Inclusion of other sources of information about teachers' proficiency including data from peers and students and self-evaluations,

- Development of a comprehensive staff development program for evaluators as well as teachers, and
- Adequate resources, time and money, to develop a thorough program of feedback and development for the staff.

Summary and Conclusions

Teacher evaluation, as the case studies and literature review indicate, is viewed as a potentially important school-based method for improving teachers' skills. In practice, however, evaluation has substantially less impact than is desired. Despite increasing emphasis on improving the quality of teacher evaluation programs, most "improvements" seem directed at formalizing procedures. As a result, regulations abound as in the states where these studies were conducted. Most teacher evaluation systems now require regular annual or biennial evaluations, specify the general performance criteria to be used, define the procedures in the evaluation cycle, call for written documentation of results, and require that those results be reviewed formally with teachers. But educators generally concur that even highly formalized evaluation systems do not help teachers, either individually or collectively, to improve their skills.

From teachers' and supervisors' perspectives, some of the changes needed to make evaluation more effective include:

- *Select methods to match the evaluation purpose.* The purpose of an evaluation system must be clearly identified and understood in order to select appropriate methods. The same procedures cannot constructively and simultaneously serve the needs of those interested in promoting teacher development and those responsible for personnel decisions. Both sets of needs are important. But different methods are needed to address different purposes.
- *Involve teachers in the evaluation.* Teachers should be involved in *all phases* of developing and operating formative systems. Any evaluation program that does not reflect the interests, concerns, aspirations, and needs of teachers is doomed to failure. By the same token, teachers must have constructive attitudes to make the system work. Teaching must be regarded as a skill to be learned and participants

must be willing managers of their own development, ready to consider, explore, and practice new teaching skills.

- *Provide relevant training.* All evaluators and staff must be thoroughly trained. Everyone involved in the evaluation should know how to use evaluation instruments to acquire useful, objective data, interpret results, and use those results to advantage. Similarly, evaluators should be trained to provide feedback to teachers that is clear, precise, and sufficiently diagnostic to promote realistic plans for improvement.

- *Increase sources of evaluation data.* Thorough formative evaluation should include the perspectives of students, peers, teachers themselves, and supervisors and incorporate several kinds of observation not just a once-a-year classroom visit.

- *Use meaningful criteria.* Performance criteria must be relevant to desired student outcomes, specific enough to be useful in planning professional development, and accepted as important by each teacher to whom they will apply.

- *Relate results to organizational goals.* Evaluation results should be used by both teachers and staff development planners to set training priorities and to evaluate success in achieving organizational and personal goals. Successful evaluation clearly is tied to organizational planning. Moreover, the system itself should be evaluated regularly before any procedures become so firmly entrenched that they are unresponsive to change.

This agenda for improvement-oriented teacher evaluation rests on one overriding assumption. That is, teachers and supervisors alike function best within an environment characterized by mutual support, and by respect and concern for personal growth and for the well being of staff members and students. Where such an environment exists, teacher evaluation offers great potential for helping teachers learn to teach better.

THREE

Case Studies of Success

We concluded our initial study with a clear set of suggestions for revising teacher evaluation systems to promote teacher development. The next logical step in the research program would have been to conduct a validity study by making the suggested changes in local evaluation systems and determining the impact of such changes on teacher improvement. Political and practical realities, however, precluded such a study. As college and regional R&D-center researchers, unaffiliated with a school district, we had no laboratory in which to validate our Study 1 results.

Therefore, in its place, we substituted a study that provided roughly equivalent information. We broadcast an inquiry to 5000 teachers across the Pacific Northwest asking any teacher who had experienced important and demonstrable professional growth as a result of a teacher evaluation to contact us so we could learn the details of their experience. Eight teachers volunteered to be interviewed. In addition, we were able to identify twenty-five additional teachers whose growth resulted from an effective evaluation through other direct inquiries with teachers. Our goal in this study was to profile the individual evaluations of these thirty-three volunteer teachers, in terms of the attributes that appeared to make them work, and compare profiles to discern those attributes common to a number of cases of effective evaluation.

Each case of growth-producing evaluation was treated as an individual event to be studied in depth. For instance, each of the eight teachers responding to the broadcast inquiry participated in an extensive structured interview designed to yield a rich description of the event. These interviews were conducted by the authors, were recorded, and were converted to verbatim transcripts. Other cases were collected by graduate students and research associates, who provided the researchers with written descriptions of the growth-producing evaluations.

In addition, in the course of conducting this research, we were able to identify two principals who had established outstanding records of conducting high-quality, growth-producing teacher evaluations. These principals also were interviewed.

In this chapter, we illustrate the nature of the case study data by providing edited transcripts of the interviews of two teachers. These particular cases were selected to illustrate as many of the key features of sound evaluation as possible. These features are noted at the right of each transcript. To accompany these, we also have included an edited transcript of one of the principal interviews. Closely examined in their entirety and considered together, these three sample cases provides an excellent lens through which to view effective teacher evaluation at work.

Our cases yielded a wide variety of factors that appear related to the productive outcome of evaluation experiences. The factors, which were identified through a systematic content analysis of teacher and principal comments, are presented in the next chapter.

Case Interview: Teacher Number One	Key Points

Researchers: Could you tell us a bit about the particular experience that caused you to respond to our inquiry, the particular positive evaluation experience?

Pat: I have had two that have really affected my life. The first one occurred in Los Angeles, California. At that time, I had been teaching about six years and the administrative assistant and principal both did the teacher evaluation. Up to that point the assistant principal came to the teacher's classroom with a checklist,

More than one supervisor was involved.

checked the room environment, quality of bulletin boards, and then discussed the follow-up procedure with you. As a new teacher, you would feel extremely uncomfortable with this. Then, after I had been teaching about six years, my assistant principal and principal both came in at different times. As a follow up, they said, "We really see some potential here." That was the first time I had had anyone approach me with that, indicating to me that perhaps I should get things moving in a different direction. So we started working together on my improvement. The principal worked with me on lesson development and lesson skills, such as teaching directive lessons. The assistant principal really worked on 'time-on-task:' "Are those children on task? If you would like me to come into your classroom, I will, and we will use a timer to actually see how many children are on task. A lot of teaching is going on but the children aren't on task."

Anxiety may result from absence of pre-conference.

Supervisors indicated that possibilities for growth exist.

Principal focused on skill development in a specific area.

Assistant principal focused on students while principal concentrated on teacher.

Assistant principal collected descriptive (non-judgmental) data.

Researcher: So they both expressed willingness to help you, to help with different parts of what you were doing?

Pat: Yes, and part of that came from me, too. Here were two really good resource people. My principal was an extremely autocratic principal. That was good because you cannot sit back. You go with what is going on or struggle with stress. His personality was strong: "These are the goals for the school, these are the goals for the district, and this is the way we are

Teacher was open to receiving assistance.

Principal expressed high expectations and school goals.

going to go." I wanted to make this a
learning experience and so it became
that type of thing for both of us.

Researcher: What is it about the principal that led you to believe that he
was a credible source of ideas or help?
What about this person led you to believe that he could help you?

Pat: At that time, I felt intimidated
and threatened, to tell you the truth,
but I work well under that kind of con-
dition. I like to be pushed. As for the
assistant principal, she was very professional looking in dress. I feel that
teaching is a profession and if you
want to be considered a professional
you better start acting like it.

    She had a professional quality that I
really admired. I talked to her about
all kinds of activities that I wanted going on in my classroom and there
were no resource people in my classroom. I wanted help. Why did I feel she
could give me that? I invited her to
teach a lesson in my classroom and I
saw exactly how I wanted my class to
be taught. There was a purpose to the
lesson, it had an opener, it was creative but structured, and the children
knew what was expected of them.
There are certain qualities that you
know intuitively. She has been my
principal for three years now. Every
experience has been positive.

*Teacher needed to be
challenged.*

*Teacher and assis-
tant principal shared
similar values.*

*Assistant principal
possessed credibility.*

*Teacher asked for
help.*

*Assistant principal
was willing to model
appropriate teaching
behaviors.*

*Assistant principal
developed a track rec-
ord of positive experi-
ences.*

Researcher: How does a principal establish credibility in the eyes of a
teacher?

Pat: One of the main things is that the principal has to develop a rapport. Before the evaluation process takes place, they are in your classroom, I mean, *really* in your classroom. My current principal comes into my classroom. Every time she does, she wants to get to know me and the students. She can spend a good 15–20 minutes getting to know what I was teaching, what my children are doing. She always leaves a message of some sort on my desk. It is important that those principals communicate what positive things they are seeing first, before they go into that interview process.

Supervisors must get to know each teacher's classroom and students.

Supervisor took an active interest in what teacher did.

Supervisor left notes for immediate feedback.

Supervisors should acknowledge positive things first.

Researcher: Going back to the LA experience, one person had offered to help you with one set of instructional factors and the other with another. What happened then?

Pat: I worked with the assistant principal in getting resource people. She gave me a list of names, units, and materials to start me off. I was not clear where I was going in math, she helped me with that. It was not a threatening situation. I never felt I was judged. I felt it was positive. When things started happening in my classroom, I knew things were headed in the right direction. Then she would say, "I think you have potential to do better things. I would like to see you go into administration. I think you need to get enrolled in an administrative program and get your masters." I thought, "I am not ready for this. I will

Teacher had access to various sources of assistance.

Assistant principal provided help without making judgments about teacher competence.

Assistant principal expressed confidence in teacher and encouraged her to grow. A mentor relationship developed.

just take classes to get up on the pay schedule." She started me going to school and working on an administrative degree.

Researcher: Going back to that specific instance, the assistant principal was going to help you with the time-on-task. She said she would come in with a timer and actually chart the time on task. How did all that evolve? Did she in fact do some observations? What resulted?

Pat: After she observed me, we met. The first thing she said was, "Do your children always work like that? I have never seen anything like that in my life. You had one student out of thirty-three that every ten minutes would get off task, but then he would go back to his work. I don't think you need to work so hard on this. Do you want to work on something else?" They got release time for me to visit other schools to see programs. They allowed me to do things that would give me information about good teaching practices.

Postobservation conference began on a positive note.

Supervisor was able to recognize teacher's strength.

The focus of postobservation conference was teacher growth, not correction of deficiencies.

Researcher: It sounds like what you worked on was as much a matter of your choice as it was a matter of something that resulted from the evaluation process that you or they thought needed to be changed. Is that generally true?

Pat: I don't think they saw that there was anything lacking. I had never heard of that. She said, "Has anyone ever come into your classroom to do this?" I said, "I don't even know what you are talking about." She exposed me to things that I had never been aware of. There are options for me beyond staying in a first-grade classroom.

Supervisor helped the teacher expand her horizons.

Researcher: Did you regard this interaction positively at the time or is it really the benefit of hindsight?

Pat: I think it is hindsight. At the time, I felt under a lot of pressure but I think I learned the most those six years. I learned a lot more about personality styles or leadership styles of principals. These administrators got things done, despite a lot of resistance from the staff. I saw a lot getting done in two years without many meetings or communication.

Benefits of supervision may not be realized immediately.

Researcher: Did the vice principal or the principal go through the steps of clinical supervision? Would they preconference, observe, and postconference?

Pat: Yes. I think it felt really comfortable talking to the assistant principal because she was not so much older than me and I admired her. She seemed so in control of herself and her emotions yet had so much knowledge, I wanted to learn.

All steps of clinical supervision were followed. No shortcuts.

Teacher respected and could identify with assistant principal.

Researcher: Was there a balance between the assistant principal who was supportive and the principal who kept nudging you?

Pat: Yes, I think that balance was probably the best thing. If it had just been him, I would have done all right because I would have been forced to go outside my school. I would have done that on my own, probably. I had reached a point when I realized that. I was not getting enough. I am not giving enough to my children. There has to be more. You don't get this in method classes. Some people don't ever sense this, but there has to be more creative ways of teaching besides opening the book. I am so tired of skills, teach this skill and that skill.

Two supervisors complement each other: one provides support, the other sets high expectations.

Teacher felt a need to improve the quality of instruction.

Researcher: What is it that served as evidence to you at this turning point when you said, "Well there's got to be more to it than this." Do you recall?

Pat: One day I sat down and looked around my classroom and I saw that everything was just nice and neat and tidy. As a new teacher I think you need a lot of structure; you feel comfortable that way. Everything is done in a precise way; we all sit down at the same time. As we get more mature in our teaching, it is not such an issue. If they do it quietly, I really don't care how they get it done. I had a chance to go visit another classroom and I said, "This is where it's at. These kids are enjoying what they are doing and it was at all different levels." To get to that point takes a really great teacher. She can move those children. They are each being programmed so well but they are enjoying what's happening. It is on their level and they are

Teachers develop in stages. What is a concern at one stage, such as structure, may not be a concern later.

Teachers benefit from access to other teachers and classrooms.

producing something. That is what I saw. I came back to my school and I looked at other classrooms in our school. We have to get on with this, and it either is going to come from you or you are going to get help with this.

Researcher: As you went through the process of growing that first six years, what evidence did you rely on to tell you whether that growth was going the way you wanted it to?

Pat: It wasn't so much inner satisfaction as getting these great pats on the back from the principal, administrator, and other people in the school who came into your room. "I really like that idea. Where did you get that?" A lot of teachers aren't willing to share. I don't know why. They stay in their classrooms. There is so much paperwork, they want to be able to share but there isn't enough time. Sharing, having administration evaluate you and tell you you are doing well. When the principal does an evaluation, saying the teacher is doing good or great, that's not enough. You had better look for specifics: "Your room environment is creative. I like what you are doing with this unit or I noticed when you were teaching math today. The way you used manipulatives to teach fractions was better than having them work out of the book. Kids get really involved."

Teacher received lots of recognition.

Teacher valued specific feedback, not gratuitous praise.

Researcher: Was that the kind of feedback you got through these early years? Did you receive specific information?

Pat: Yes. I got that from the assistant principal. If I hadn't received that from her, I don't know where I'd have gotten positive feedback. Teachers need to get it from somebody at the administrative level. Maybe there are other opportunities to get positive rewards outside of the classroom, but we still need great teachers and we need to let teachers know that they are doing a super job. Even those that are adequate or minimal need to hear how well they are doing, "Look, this is great. Last week this wall was blank, but it really looks neat today. I like it." The principal would do that. In fact, he would say, "Oh, you are wearing a skirt today. That looks a lot better than those levis with the patch." Teachers in California were wearing levis every day. I think the principal should evaluate teachers in and around the classroom instead of calling them into the office. They don't do that. Why don't they do that? Is it threatening to the principal? The principal would be able to pull out Johnny's workbook and say, "I noticed today that this was going on," but they don't do that.

Researcher: You mentioned earlier that you had a good experience with your current principal. How does she compare with the combination down in LA, the principal and assistant principal?

Pat: I think she is in the classroom more often than they were. They were mostly in your classroom on a term

Recognition is important to teachers.

Teacher preferred to meet with supervisor on her "turf."

By meeting in teacher's room, supervisor has access to samples of student work.

Supervisor visited the classroom frequently.

basis to evaluate you. She tries to come in at least once a week. When she comes in she always leaves some kind of message or note on your desk. It's not an evaluation. So whenever evaluation time comes, you can feel comfortable. She has already let you know what her expectations are, what she feels, whether you are doing what is on task, or whatever. She lets you know what she expects from you when you walk in your classroom. She did this in a staff meeting.

And she left a note with impressions.

The final evaluation was never a surprise because supervisor's periodic notes let teacher know how she felt and what she expected.

Researcher: Does she do that through implication, formal presentations, listing things that are her priorities? Does she let you know in some other ways?

Pat: Only on an informal basis and at the preconference does she let you know the major areas. Teaching and learning are extremely important to the classroom environment. How does she do this? She comes into your classroom and leaves notes. Then she calls you into the office for the preconference. "Now, I would like you to make out your goals and objectives for the year." She wants you to be specific. She lets you choose. This year she wanted math to be one of them because the district is pushing that we do a good job in the area of math. So I did that and met with her again. She told me she would come in twice. She lets me choose the time. I prefer that I don't. I like it when it is unexpected because then you teach better everyday. The day after they come in for

During preconference, supervisor had teacher think about the entire year and set goals.

Supervisor linked teacher development to school and district goals.

Teacher can select time for supervisor visit, but this teacher preferred not to know.

evaluations, you are relaxed. She comes in the classroom and she stays. A good evaluation is going to be two hours. How is the principal going to do it? If they want to know where their teachers are, it is two hours. They say sometimes the principal will know by walking by the room, but you don't know. Some teachers have very little on the board but they are really teaching those kids.

Teacher feels two hours is necessary for a thorough evaluation.

Researcher: How much time does your supervisor spend in the observation?

Pat: I had 180 minutes last year. That was my first year. But it varies.

Researcher: Is it more than a few minutes?

Pat: Oh, yes. She comes in and sits down for a good hour and if I am teaching reading, she gets right into the reading group. The first time she came in for science I wasn't nervous, I wasn't uncomfortable, but I said, "I need help with this one group and can you help?" It worked out well because she could see that the kids were involved in this one activity where they took a bird's nest apart and categorized what they found. It was at their level, and they could do it. She found out some new things. So if teachers would feel comfortable doing that, principals might enjoy that. It is very hard for them to write down what they are seeing, but she managed to do it. She stayed for that time. It is

Supervisor spent a long block of time observing. She participated in the lesson.

Supervisor gained firsthand knowledge of teacher's students by working with them.

important when the principal comes in that they smile. The children shouldn't talk to them. They can't be too obvious but they should smile. First of all, that makes the teacher feel more comfortable.When my former administrator came in you felt very comfortable. You wanted to show off because she made you feel good. I have always had a positive experience. I know she is working with one of our staff members on some kind of program and she meets with him for breakfast once a week to try and get things going. I know the evaluation there hasn't been too good but she is following up.

Supervisor should appear congenial when visiting class.

Researcher: How do you come to know of a teacher being on a plan of assistance? Is it common knowledge?

Pat: It is when the children are in the hall and all over the place and you see the principal meet with that person once a week. No one says anything, but you know.

Stigma is attached to being on a plan of assistance.

You put two and two together. It is unfortunate. I see all this coming from the administrator, trying to help this person. I feel the best way to do it is to say, "Look, Joe, you are having a hard time. You know what I am going to do." Some school districts and some states pull out teachers to serve as teacher evaluation assistants to work with new teachers and teachers in trouble, to bring them up. If they don't make it after so many weeks, then that is it. Or, pair older teachers with new teachers. My former admin-

Teachers helped other teachers.

istrator did that. I learned so much. I was with a teacher of 54 and I was 26 at the time.

Researcher: Talk more about that experience. How did that all come about?

Pat: That was initiated by the principal. It was an older staff. He wanted a reading program. We were used to the basal. He believed that kindergarten should not just be readiness. Those children who are ready to read should be reading. That is what he wanted, so he put me into kindergarten with a teacher. He put those of us who were more progressive with those who had been teaching kindergarten a long time, doing a fine job the way they were doing it. There were some complaints from parents because the child has been in preschool for two years and he was still doing nursery rhymes and cut and pasting. Maybe they could learn to write their name? So we worked together. I was lucky, because I was with Ann. She was really opinionated and I thought this wasn't going to work. But it turned out to be wonderful. I didn't try to force anything. We would get into philosophical differences. Like, "Ann, I really think they need to be taking homework home. Let them cut the alphabet out of magazines. The parents could help." "No, I think we should do that in art. Let's just have the painting station over here and when they finish their work we could do this much alphabet." I had an afternoon

Teacher modeling can be very instructive, particularly when it occurs in the new teacher's own class.

and she had a morning session and we would each help each other for an hour. So I got to see what she was doing, then I did what I wanted to do.

Researcher: Are you the kind of person who has a sense of where you need to grow, even in the absence of feedback from the principal?

Pat: Yes, I am having a terrible time right now. I think I am the best teacher I could ever be. I think I could go into any classroom, in any situation, and really do a good job. I need to grow. I would like to get out of the classroom. I would like to be working with teachers in the district. I would like to be doing in-service.

Teacher had very high expectations, a need to grow, and a willingness to help others.

Researcher: Just a couple more questions about your current evaluation process. Is it ever the case, that in her notes your supervisor would suggest changes you might make things you might do differently, or is it always positive kinds of things?

Pat: She once said, "I noticed you had a lot of trouble getting into this one activity and then I went and looked at the test scores and they looked really low." As a result of that comment, I read those test scores more than I ever have in the beginning of the year. As a result of that one little comment, pre- and posttesting is really important to me in their achievement levels. I tend to take everything so personally. People tell me not to be so sensitive about it.

Teacher views constructive suggestions as beneficial, not critical.

Researcher: Do most view the evaluation process as a source of growth or do they view it as a waste of time?

Pat: A waste of time. "I have to go through this. I better get a bulletin board up," that type of thing. A ritual. The more experienced teachers really don't care. It is the new teachers that it is important for. It really gets them going.

There is a need to distinguish the type of evaluation used with new and with experienced teachers.

Researcher: Thank you for your time.

Case Interview: Teacher Number Two

Key Points

Researcher: Please share the positive experience you have had with an evaluation/supervisor. What were the details?

Ken: The principal made it very clear, first of all, what was expected of me. She would give immediate feedback in very descriptive terms. Sometimes I didn't want to hear them. "So-and-so was up four times during the time I was in the room observing, apparently for no reason." Or she gave me a good outline of ways to approach a lesson: making sure that I had an anticipatory setup for the kids; that the objectives were clearly stated, what the students were expected to do; and that at the end of the lesson there was some sort of closure. I think that's definitely a given for an evaluation, that you have a clear idea of where a

Principal communicated clear expectations. Principal provided immediate feedback using descriptive (nonjudgmental) data.

Principal offered useful suggestions for improving practice.

Principal was guided by a clear model of good instruction.

lesson begins, how it goes from the beginning through the end and how to close it. I think that is a big help to students and to teachers for the administrators to lay those rules out for the teachers.

I really think it should be done in the fall, rather than as we do here. This is April and now it is permanent teacher evaluation time. The evaluation process should start in the fall. If the expectations of the administrator are made very clear and there are achieveable things that teachers can do, then that's one of the ways that the evaluation becomes positive.

Model of instruction was shared early in school year.

The other thing that was done at our school, was to bring in help. The principal brought in help from the outside. In this particular case, it happened to be a clinical psychologist. He was mostly concerned with the teacher—student interaction and he had some simple guidelines that he had gleaned from literature in terms of the best way to deal with kids. He was a very good person. He sat in on my classes two or three times and he modeled himself, in dealing with me and with other teachers, the way he felt people should deal with students.

Principal utilized outside resources to help teachers improve.

Researcher: What caused the principal to invite this person to come in?

Ken: Well, the first year I was at this school, the principal was new, too. The previous principal had left behind several years of benign neglect. Teachers had done whatever they felt they should do—as teachers will, when there isn't a strong administrator. The new principal's approach was to bring uniformity into teaching. There would be a clear idea on the part of all the teachers on how to deal with the students, so that when students went from class to class, they wouldn't be subjected to some of the arbitrary kinds of things teachers do. By bringing the psychologist in, she was modeling for everyone how she thought teachers should deal with students. There was a little opposition to it, but not a whole lot of it. Most of the people were very competent already. It's just that they had gotten into some bad habits.

In particular, she was concerned with the bussing program. We had a few kids bussed in from the inner city. She wanted to make sure that they were dealt with on a fair basis. It is my understanding that it hadn't happened before, but that's only secondhand. I wasn't there, when she came. As a new leader, so to speak, she wanted to make sure that everyone knew what was expected and she brought the psychologist in. He presented workshops on ways of measuring student behavior, suggestions for things, such as doing a perception check to see who is on task and who is not or other methods of making sure that you know what is going on. His contention was that kids are on task a lot more often than they are not on task, but the teachers tend to pick the times when the kids aren't on task and exaggerate them into major conflicts. That isn't a wise thing to do at all.

Principal sought to create a common understanding of good practice among all staff members.

Researcher: When you first began your working relationship with the new principal, what was your impression of her in terms of her value as a source of information for you? Was she a credible source of information? Did you anticipate a positive evaluation?

Ken: Oh, I think so. The first time I talked to her, she was very positive. I went down to see her when I found out that I was at her school. They moved several grades to that school and they asked me to go along. So when I talked to her, she said, "Hey, the parents from there are excited about having you come to help with the transition." So there were positive expectations right from the beginning. Then, when problems developed, she was very specific about what the problems were and occasionally outspoken about the problems. She is like most good principals, very strong willed with a very clear idea of how school should take place. She was always very adamant about making sure that you understood that if things weren't going the way that they should, then she had suggestions about things to do to make it better.

Principal started off on a positive note.

Principal communicated concerns in very specific terms.

Principal always offered suggestions when a problem was identified.

Researcher: Do you recall the specific ways she did this? Which things changed as a result of interactions with her?

Ken: I think the key thing in the interactions with this principal was the idea that every lesson should begin with some kind of clear statement to the kids about what is expected. For example, when we begin a lesson, the title of the lesson is on the board. What I have done in the past, although not recently, is have a ditto for them on the table while I am taking the attendance. They would read through this as to what they are going to do today. "Open your book to such-and-such a page," or "We're going to see a film," or "You are going to do the experiment on this page." So the kids know exactly what is expected of them. There is none of this, "What are we going to do today?" or "I don't understand."

The second thing I think she gave was a lot of help and encouragement in writing clear objectives for lessons, not necessarily sophisticated behavioral objectives, but measurable objectives. "Students will be able to name the layers of the earth. Students will be able to tell you two or three facts about each layer," or goals at the higher level, although it's always hard to come up with measurable goals for some of the higher level things.

If we had a problem, there never was a "We'll deal with that next week," or "Let me think about it, I'll get back to you." It was always very quick. Sometimes the solution wasn't what you wanted to hear, but the feedback was always there. The key things were knowing what her expectations were and knowing that she was going to support you and allow you to grow. Previous to that, I had had the standard kind of evaluation experiences, which had not been very meaningful at all. I was just swimming along, try-

Principal offered encouragement along with suggestions. She didn't just leave the teacher to "sink or swim."

ing to be successful and doing as well as I could. I never really had enough training. I got into teaching by the back door. I don't know if that makes a difference, but I had a liberal arts degree, in political science.

Evaluation and training may have to make up for past deficits.

I had been involved in teaching for eleven years. And part of that time was in the East, something different than here. There, you weren't allowed to write objectives for your classes, the union wouldn't permit it at that time. I don't know if it is still true, but it was true then. The principal asked me to write behavioral objectives for my science class. Next thing I knew there was a union rep at my door. "You can't do that. And you are not responsible for what those kids learn." That was about the time I decided it was time to come back to the West. It was getting out of hand there and I'm afraid it probably still is.

Context of labor— management relations can make a difference in teacher evaluation experience.

Researcher: Can we talk about the observation process that you were involved in? Did she tend to observe just at one time?

Ken: Whenever she came into your room, you knew she was observing. You always knew that she knew what was going on. She had that aura about her. She had it with the kids. I used to kid her and say she could frost a whole cafeteria just by coming in and giving a stare and she could do that with the teachers, too, sometimes. When she was mad—this didn't happen very often—you knew it. She felt she had good reasons for it.

Evaluator possessed credibility as an observer and instructional leader.

Principal was able to express dissatisfaction as well as give recognition.

Researcher: So she followed the standard clinical supervision cycle?

Ken: Yes. That's prescribed here in the contract. It has to be done that way.

Principal followed the clinical supervision cycle.

Researcher: Were there other less formal things that went on also?

Ken: Yes, very much so. If she happened to go by your room, walking in the hallway and she saw something that was confusing, she would call you in and talk to you. "What was going on here?" or "Why did this happen?" or "You sent this student out for referral. What can you do about that?" or "This kid has got a problem. Try to deal with it this way." There was always that support. Lots of contact with her. We only had about 160 sixth, seventh, and eighth graders with eight teachers. A little different than trying to run a middle school. She had the kindergarten through fifth grade, also, but essentially, we were running two separate programs.

Other things she did were to start the continuous progress program that we still have here, which was a big help. She had a lot of innovative ideas that made it an exciting place to be and she was the reason I came here, or one of the reasons. Without her help, I probably would have been successful, but as I said, focusing in and getting the support made you feel that it was valuable to you to do what she wanted. Sometimes by withholding support, she made it clear that

Principal made frequent informal visits to classrooms.

Principal dealt with concerns immediately rather than letting them accumulate.

School size may play a role in supervisor's effectiveness.

Principal developed a reputation for innovative ideas that led to improved instruction.

Principal focused on specific concerns, not

you had done something wrong, but she never made it a personality thing. She never made you feel that you were not a valuable part of the staff.

on an individual's character.

Researcher: You certainly have described attributes of that principal that helped you grow. After eleven years of experience, most people would regard you as a seasoned professional. What attributes do you have that allowed for the kind of change that took place?

Ken: My expectations would have something to do with it. My expectations are very high. What I expect to have happen in class is for every student to earn an *A*. In order to do that, you've got to set up a lesson that is going to meet the needs of every single student and I still feel that can be done. I am not nearly to that point now, but I am always willing to have someone make any suggestions about what happens in my room. I am always willing to try something new. Maybe someday, I will be able to say that I've got a perfect system. I just don't have that now. I see kids that I'm not reaching for one reason or another. There aren't very many of those, but even one is too many. That is one of the reasons I am here, I think, because it's a more challenging place to be and it's easier to see kids with special needs. When you reach those kids a little bit, it's very rewarding. I guess it is an ego-type thing. I get strokes for myself by trying to improve what I do. If I ever get to the

Teacher had high personal expectations.

Teacher was open to new ideas.

Teacher was always striving to do better, and to grow.

Teacher was exhilarated by challenge.

point where I think I've got the perfect system, then it will be time to do something else. So I guess that's a characteristic of me. I am always trying to improve, trying to grow, trying to change.

Teacher took risks.

Researcher: Have you had experiences during your career where the people conducting the evaluation process didn't contribute much to your growth?

Ken: Yes. In fact, it got to the point where their hands were tied literally, because the union would not allow them to support me. Essentially, it became, "Oh, you are doing a fantastic job." I knew I wasn't and it was a lot of hollow praise. Maybe I was doing a fantastic job considering what other people were doing, but you know that's not so good. I have had people tell me, "You are a good science teacher." My response to that is, "In the country of the blind, the one-eyed man is king." Especially now, I think we have a lot of good science teachers, but back East it was easy to be really good at it because most people just go through the motions. That's not true here, not true at all. Maybe it's just a fact that I do need help, while there is a lot of room for improvement. I find it hard to remember to do all of the things that my supervisor taught me. I need the reinforcement and we don't get as much here as I would like. It's one of the problems with a big school. There aren't enough strokes given. That's one of the problems in teach-

Teacher resented gratuitous praise. He felt the union prevented meaningful evaluation from occurring.

Context makes a difference.

Teacher could use more encouragement and recognition.

ing in general, and it is probably true for administrators as well. There aren't enough times when somebody says "Hey, good job."

I wanted to share my positive experience for two reasons. First of all, I thought her model for evaluation was a really good one and the key thing is an interpersonal relationship, the human equation. The key in any relationship between adults and between adults and students is the human relationship. She was a very human individual with human failings, as well as good qualities. She was always there to support what you did and if you did something wrong, the reprimand you were given was always done in a positive way. The support was there, but something was wrong and you needed to do something.

The key to good evaluation is the relationship between supervisor and teacher.

Principal could deliver criticism in a constructive way.

Researcher: Did you appreciate her more in retrospect or at the time were you also appreciative of her?

Ken: That is an excellent point. There were times when we really thought, "Here she comes again!" But afterwards, when I came over here, I saw that using what she had taught me made it easier for me. She taught me things to do that no one else ever had bothered to tell me to do, even though I taught for eleven years and was successful. She showed that you have the potential for growth, you could do better. She did that with the kids.

Appreciation for supervisor may build over time. It takes time for suggestions to be tested and to prove useful.

Principal was able to provide growth opportunities for veterans.

Researcher: You have described the impact that she had on you. But, could you see an impact on the kids as you were changing, as you were instituting new ideas? What evidence did you have that they were benefiting?

Ken: One of the key things was not in science, which I was teaching part time, but in language arts where I had the next to the bottom group. She suggested that we go with a certain program in corrective reading. She encouraged me to go to Eugene for the workshop. I came back and we implemented the program, which was very teacher-directed. I had one kid in there that didn't want to do it. The minute she saw her response it was very simple. "We'll change her into a different group." She didn't say to me, "You've got to make this kid do it. Why can't you make this kid do it?" She pulled the kid out. Those were the kinds of things she would do. She thought that was best for the student, too.

Principal encouraged teacher to visit other schools and see recommended programs in action.

Principal provided ongoing support during implementation of new program.

Researcher: The program was effective for that group of students?

Ken: The program was very effective. The kids showed lots of growth. We put a little money into it in terms of rewards. When they did a certain assignment, or certain number of assignments, they got to go bowling, ice skating, out for pizza, or they earned pencils, magic markers, or coloring books. She supported that also. There was a lot of growth on the part of the kids. So the kids liked the program a lot. There were other things involved

Principal's suggested program passed the "acid test"—it helped kids. Such success adds to the principal's credibility.

in the program, too, but the main thrust was student comprehension.

Researcher: What effect did that kind of evaluation, that kind of growth producing process, have on other teachers in the organization as a whole?

Ken: Outside of our school? Probably not much. I don't know what principals do, whether they share things about evaluation with each other. In this building, the evaluation has been a sore subject because it has been abused in some cases, I think. There were evaluations done by one evaluator. Then another evaluator would come in to do a much different evaluation on the same person, teaching the same class in the same way. I have never been evaluated by our current principal. This is the third year he has been here. I was evaluated by his personnel assistant the first year that he was here.

Current principal does not follow regular evaluation routine.

Researcher: Do you think most other teachers expect the evaluation process to contribute to professional development?

Ken: It is rather hard to speak for other people but I would think so, yes. I think most teachers are looking for someone to come in and say, "I like this, this, and this and I have some questions about this. What exactly are you trying to do here? I saw this happening in the classroom and I think if you tried this instead, you might be more successful." It's very

Teachers welcome information about their performance.

hard to communicate those skills to other people, and that is why she is so successful, because she could do that. She would come in and model lessons for you if you wished.

Principal was able to model desirable teaching behaviors.

Researcher: Did you get a chance to watch her in action?

Ken: Yes. She had some very clear ideas about how to evaluate kids, how to make up tests, how to keep records of growth. She was always trying to pile up things the district had. The Teachers' Association would get very upset about the big checklists of skills, which were really good, but they were a lot of work. "Ken has mastered spelling words that follow the rule, change the *y* to *i* and add the *es.*" That's how specific they were, fourth-grade level skills, fifth-grade level skills. She suggested that we keep track of those kinds of things as much as possible. She tried to show us easy ways to do it. "Develop one or two test items for a given skill. Don't give them a big test on twenty-five words that end in *y.* The kid knows how to do it. They are going to know how to do it with three of four words on any other skill." She wasn't doing it just for the sake of making work for people, but tried to show people that if you are going to evaluate students, you have got to have some specific goals with specific goal-oriented test items. That was the same approach she used with teachers. Her goal was to improve teaching and she had some ideas that she thought were good. Now, for the

Principal had lots of suggestions for improving instruction.

Classroom achievement data play a role in teacher growth.

Principal's purpose in supervision was improving instruction.

people that already were excellent teachers, she didn't expect them to change in any way. But I think everybody at Hayhurst thought that they were excellent due to her being there. The humanistic environment was part of that.

Teachers identified with the principal and took pride in her leadership.

You're not going to have a real successful teaching environment unless you trust that the administrator has your best interest in mind. I don't think you're really going to be that excited about listening to what the person has to say about your performance and be willing to do what that administrator suggests to you.

Trust is a key to productive supervision.

Researcher: The crucial step then is for the administrator to establish that trust, to establish the fact that you can trust them?

Ken: Yes.

Researcher: What are the keys to doing that in your opinion? How can supervisors best do that from a teacher's perspective?

Ken: They have got to be honest in what they do. They have to say, "This is who I am and these are my ideas about how school should be. I think I am going to come around to see what you do and I'm going to support whatever you do that I think is positive with the kids. I am going to ask you for ideas too, on how to make things better. We'll work together to try and make this school as good as possible." Some teachers often approach the

Honesty and clear expectations are keys to trust.

Supervisors need to value teachers' ideas.

current administrator looking for a hidden agenda, looking for people to take his place on the job, that kind of thing. Someone tries to be the principal, instead of just being the teacher. Those suspicions are still there. They'll always be there, and it's too bad, because I think that anyone who becomes a principal must have good skills. They probably have had a successful teaching experience.

It would be nice if they could be taught to communicate their skills to other people, if they don't already know how to do that. The other thing is that the evaluations should start in the fall. It should begin at day one. You've got to talk to and look at people in September. If they are doing great, tell them they are doing great. It's a joke to talk to people in April, especially if you think something is negative. It's a little late in April to worry about that. So that's a problem the way the contract is written up.

Principals need to be able to communicate what they know about instruction. Knowing it is insufficient.

Effective supervision begins early in the fall.

I suppose the way the contract is now is that the principal has to evaluate permanent teachers by May 1 every other year. It doesn't say that they couldn't do it before that. But I guess that principals would argue that they have a heavy workload already and it would be just too burdensome for them.

Researcher: Or else there are some teachers that the principals assume are doing a fine job, and they concentrate on ones that they are more worried about.

Ken: Yes. There is always room for improvement, always things that you can do. The other problem that can happen is that you have a principal whose management and teaching style is something you don't want to have anything to do with. Then you have a real problem, because you have to watch out so that you won't end up being like this person. A teacher has to be able to separate out what's good and what's not good about principals, just as principals have to be able to separate out those things for teachers. There are people who get by, or become successful teachers by putting the kids down, being essentially cruel in the "best interest" of the children. I can't do that. It's not my style.

Teacher judgment plays a role in supervisory relations.

Researcher: So you would be less apt to give any credibility to that person?

Ken: It's a little hard to take anything seriously that somebody tells you about teaching, when you don't like the way they deal with kids.

How a supervisor deals with students helps determine his or her credibility with teachers.

Researcher: Good point. Thanks for talking with us.

Case Interview: A Supervisor

Key Points

Researcher: Can you think of teachers you supervised who grew professionally as a result of your evaluation of their performance?

Linda: First, I need to put those individual cases in context with some of the other things I did to improve instruction in one particular building where I worked. I spent a lot of time on staff development, classroom management, lesson planning—long-range, short-range—selecting appropriate instructional activities in language arts, science, and in a limited way, mathematics. I spent a tremendous amount of time, almost every staff meeting, dealing with those kinds of issues over the four years that I was there. There were a lot of initial instructions to teachers about what my expectations were in terms of their performance in the classroom and also instructions related to how to do a better job of teaching language arts and science. After discussing these things in staff meetings, I spent a lot of time making classroom observations, very informal observations.

A growth-producing teacher evaluation does not take place in a vacuum. It depends on many factors, such as opportunities for staff development.

Staff meetings focused on instruction. School climate was identified with instructional improvement.

Most days I made a circuit of all the classrooms and I specially focused my time observing the language arts classes, which was where we were putting our primary instructional emphasis. I worked in a school that had lower-achieving kids, where there was a real need to improve in that particular area. I got a lot of data about what each teacher was doing in relation to my expectations for their performance. I would use that information. I would see things they were doing well and things that I thought needed improvement.

Much time was spent in classrooms. Informal observations were more important than formal observations.

As I picked up this information, I tried to find a way to share this infor-

Observation data were shared with teachers

mation with the teacher, either casually over lunch, by dropping by after school for five minutes, or I might wait a week for a more opportune time to talk. I might collect data over a period of several days or weeks until I was able to see some kind of pattern that I wanted to sit down and work on with them.

in an informal way.

Researcher: Was this the formal evaluation?

Linda: No. I also did the formal evaluations, observations and conferences where I would sit down for a specified period of time, take a verbatim text of what was going on, analyze that text, and then have a formal evaluation with the teacher. Those happened so rarely. The formal evaluation is very time consuming. They're not frequent enough for me so I needed to combine that with lots of little mini-observations.

Formal observations require a great deal of time.

Researcher: In the course of doing that, did you combine the formal and informal, or were they separate systems?

Linda: No, in my mind they were all mixed together. I just went through the formal procedure because I had to do it. Writing it all down on paper to hand in to the district office had less value to me than ongoing conversations with teachers about what they were doing. All the information I got from watching them teach, I could use to plan the kind of staff development that was needed for individual teachers or groups of teachers. The formal evaluation part was helpful in the sense that it was my way of reinforcing teachers for things they did well in relation to the expectations I had for instruction.

Formal evaluation was viewed as an opportunity for reinforcement, not an occasion to identify problems.

One year, we really focused in on long range planning. The teachers took the curriculum continuum, all their diagnostic assessment information on students in their classes, and made some judgments about the skills they were going to focus on. They selected appropriate instructional materials for teaching those skills. We really spent a lot of time and effort on that. Over the year, when I was evaluating teachers and I was focusing in on something in staff development, you would see that coming up on all their evaluation forms. It was a way of reinforcing them for working hard. I always linked everything I did in staff development to formal evaluations. "These are some of the things I will be looking for in the formal evaluation." It acquired a formal feel of accountability. "Somebody is going to be checking, this is what they are going to be looking for, and if I do a good job, have difficulty, or don't do well in these areas, I should expect to see that on my evaluation form." I assume people would have thought that they would have seen something negative.

Researcher: Were there aspects of the informal discussion of instruction improvement that didn't appear in the formal evaluation?

Linda: Oh, yes. You can't possibly write everything that you are doing in that formal evaluation.

Formal evaluation is too brief to permit a review of all important issues.

Researcher: Were there characteristics of people or instruction or aspects of performance that you chose to deal with in the informal review that you didn't deal with in the formal review?

Linda: I'm sure there were but I can't sort that out.

Researcher: If that is the case, it would be interesting to know what caused you to want to make something public and deal with something else privately.

Linda: I would say many things that were negative or could be viewed as negative, such as the teacher's style, were private communication. I had a teacher in my building who would get angry and pop off at other staff members every once in a while about me. I had to talk to her about that particular style of communication and how I would like her to get a grip on it. I did not include that in the formal evaluation. She did do something about it. If this had been a serious problem and she had not done something about it after I had talked to her about it, then that might have been something that I would have included. There is a section there on communicating with staff.

Principal did not avoid confronting teachers with concerns, but it was done outside the context of formal evaluation.

Researcher: Some administrators will cover themselves at the first indica-

tion of a problem. They record it formally so it doesn't come back to haunt
them in the future. It is as if you are
giving this individual the benefit of
the doubt, allowing it to go unrecord-
ed in the formal evaluation system the
first time because behavior was cor-
rected.

Linda: I told my staff that if I saw a
problem with instruction, how they
were disciplining children, or how
they were working with other people, I
would always discuss that with them
first and they would know about it.
There would be an opportunity to address that. It would never pop up in a
formal evaluation as a surprise.

*Trust was generated
by ensuring staff that
cocerns will be dis-
cussed before they are
recorded on an evalu-
ation form.*

I deal with issues very directly with
teachers. If I saw a problem in the
classroom or if they were having a
problem with other staff or a problem
with me, I talked to them about it
right away and asked them to do
something about it. There were usually changes in the positive direction.
Some were chronic. They would keep
doing it. In talking with teachers, I
looked at that in a positive way. I
didn't look at it as a tool for enforce-
ment—that if you don't do something
right I can get you and I will get you.
Even though you may not be doing
that, a formal evaluation still has that
hold on people. But, I tended to look
positively. I often questioned whether
I shouldn't have put some more negative things in.

*Problems tended to be
defined as opportuni-
ties.*

Researcher: It sounds as if the informal observation may have less of that

power connotation. There is a different kind of communication going on at that time. Is that true?

Linda: Yes. The informal might be more nerve wracking because I am there all the time. I am always watching and looking. I will probably always talk to you about what I see happening. Initially, teachers might be more comfortable with the formal evaluation process because it doesn't happen very often. In the informal process someone is paying a lot of attention to instruction and that person is never going to go away. So it is much more involving. If you are giving information to a teacher that is helpful, or if you are helping a teacher to perceive things in a new way and instruction improves or discipline improves, the teacher feels better and is happier. They feel good about it. I never had a grievance come out of these informal conferences. There may be some growling, but I didn't hear about that.

Frequent classroom visits are valued when teachers actually see instruction improve.

Researcher: How did you decide who and what to observe? You said already that you had certain high-priority areas and you would spend time there. You tried to make the circuit every day. Were there any particular things that you looked for?

Linda: Just about every day, I did try to make a circuit. Two of the teachers I used to miss all the time were the PE teacher and the music teacher, because my focus tended to be on the

When the principal is in the classrooms every day, there is less likelihood small con-

basic skills. I would forget and they also were in an enclosed area. I was always conscientious about the other teachers, spreading myself around fairly equally. But, yes, I spent more time observing certain teachers who were having difficulty and I would also watch them more frequently during the day. I might watch all the teachers in language arts and then come back to teachers who were having more trouble in language arts, at transition times or lunch time. I would be watching them more frequently to see what was happening and to get a better feel for where their problems were occurring. Were they having trouble getting kids to make transitions from one activity to another? How were they managing their math programs in relation to how they were managing their language programs?

There is one teacher that I will talk to you about because it is kind of a case study. I will try to recall exactly what I observed. In my first year there, she had tremendous difficulty with student management, kids were coming out of her room during the day, almost every day. I would have four or five children sent to the office and when I would go in to observe her lessons, many children were off task, being rude, not working on instructional activities appropriate for them. She was having difficulty with a lot of things. But she was very conscientious and willing to learn. I worked with this teacher several days every week with fairly frequent daily observations, frequent conferences after

cerns will grow into big problems.

Observations were purposeful even when done informally.

school. In the spring of that first year, I was afraid I might have to take some action in terms of encouraging her to leave the profession.

Researcher: Did you voice these concerns to her?

Linda: Yes. In the spring we talked about it in terms of my needing to see some improvement. I worked a lot with her on planning skills, diagnosing student needs, developing strategies for handling behavior management with kids.

Principal was honest about her concerns.

Then, that summer, she took a class at a local college and the next year she came back significantly improved. I think she learned a lot from the class. I think she had picked up skills in planning from the year before. The following year she really started to implement confidently many of the planning skills that we had worked on. In fact, she became one of the teachers there that I would choose to teach other teachers how to do that planning. She completely turned around as a teacher. Her voice tone is very flat and monotonous and she has difficulty varying her pace with children. Even though she will do a good job of planning, developing good activities, and diagnosing kids well, she will still have difficulty losing kids with that kind of personal style. She has control of her classroom and is a good teacher and planner. She made a tremendous change and part of that was related to supervision and a lot of support and encouragement.

Teachers are capable of improvement, and even marginal teachers can become excellent.

Change is more likely when it is accompanied by support and encouragement.

Researcher: When you say "support," are you talking about anything besides verbal support?

Linda: Yes, help with lesson plans, help with behavior. I helped write behavior contracts for students. If students had trouble in their class, I worked with them as well. I help develop reinforcement plans for them. I would take a kid out, see how he is doing, see what his problems were academically.

Support includes practical suggestions and modeling

Researcher: Many principals seem unwilling or unable to provide that type of specific assistance.

Linda: It may be that my being able to provide that assistance took a lot of the fear out of my coming in to observe. I talked to the teacher about what is going on in the classroom and I always followed observations with things that we could do. I would think of some things; she would think of some things. It was a team effort, sitting down working together. My whole purpose was to have that classroom run smoothly, the teacher do a good job, the kids learn so they feel good about themselves. And I was willing to work with that teacher to help get her or him there.

Collaboration is a key.

Researcher: It's not just leadership. We distinguish between leadership and technical expertise. Leadership is important but you also have the technical expertise to understand instructional design.

An effective supervisor needs to possess instructional expertise.

Linda: I know. I don't know how to be very clear about these things, but I am sure it has something to do with sensitivity to people. A lot of the conferences between the principal and teacher relies on your sensitivity to that teacher's particular feelings at the time, what they are able to hear you say or not hear, or how much you are going to help them improve instruction, how many things you have to work on at one time. It is a personal thing.

An effective supervisor also needs to be sensitive to people's individual needs.

Researcher: In the particular case you described, can you remember any of the sensitivities that had to come into play for that particular individual?

Linda: It's been so long I can't remember. I was very positive. "These are the things I see. I think we can do something about this. Let me get you this. It sure went better today." Very positive and helpful rather than pretty intense. When I see something going well, when I see a teacher having difficulty, I always tell them about it. I always give a lot of positive reinforcement. We are supposed to start off mentioning positive things, then eventually the teacher will be more open about having trouble. I make sure there is both positive and negative.

Researcher: Some principals don't have a conception of what, in the best of all possible worlds, teachers should be doing. Our theory is that lots of principals don't spend time in the classroom because they don't know what to look for. They can be excellent communicators and they can be very sensitive, but somewhere along the line they were encouraged to be managers, not instructional leaders and they just don't know what good instruction looks like. Do you agree?

Linda: To support what you are saying, I have changed tremendously in what I have been able to see in classrooms now compared to when I started. My skill level is much, much higher now. I just did an observation of a teacher who is having difficulty at an elementary school. I took lengthy verbatim textbook plans in the classroom and I had one shot to work with this guy. After the recent work that I have done on principles of learning and curriculum planning, I know the content subject matter well, know the strategies for teaching really well. When I went in to observe this teacher, I was more able to be specific and precise about some things that could be changed or improved. I remember when I first went in to observe, I got a general sense of whether things were going well or not, and I had some fairly general ideas of what could be done to improve it. But the more I learn, the more capable I am of zeroing in on what is the real problem or concern, or what is going well. Also, I have a much larger repertoire of things that I can do to help that person. I don't quite know how you go in and supervise a teacher without that kind of instructional background.

Being an effective supervisor requires constant reading and development. Supervisors, like teachers, must continue to grow.

A strong instructional background is essential.

Researcher: We would be interested in your opinion about the possibility that someone other than the principal may need to be the supervisor or may be a source of valued information.

Linda: Yes. I have teachers watch how other teachers are teaching. They gave me feedback on other teachers. For instance, I was working with one of my less able teachers. When I was not there, the team leader would observe and report back. One of the problems you have as an administrator is that sometimes the kids will change when you come in. They suddenly will behave themselves. In these cases, other teachers are better able to see the real behavior.

Teachers can offer valuable advice to other teachers.

Researcher: From a perspective of measuring teacher performance, that's one of the major technical measurement problems to address. Preplanned performance may not be typical. The best possible performance is being observed in the traditional accountability-oriented evaluation.

Linda: This is where informal evaluations help.

Researcher: Can you tell us about a teacher you have helped in that way?

Linda: One new teacher was very insecure about getting any help from me. I left him alone for the first year. I helped on general staff development. It wasn't an emergency situation, as it was with the first woman I described. We discussed ways for doing long-range planning, my expectations, kinds of activities he should be using, and what he should be doing with assessment, etc. He was one of those people who really didn't put a lot of effort into implementing anything or really trying it.

In my second year, I started holding conferences with him more often. I worked with him on behavior management, which would improve for a period of time and drop off as soon as I dropped off. Then it would pick back up as I came in to make more intensive observations. Some improvements were made but nothing major. I eventually got to the point, in my third or fourth year, in which I met with him a lot and provided more individualized conferences where we sat down and did some planning together. His plans improved somewhat but I still wasn't pleased enough with him. So, that summer, I came up with a plan. I did his lesson plans for two months. He wasn't able, at least not with my help at the time, to modify the standard instructional program to fit the needs of his kids so I did it and had him use it. Then I had him gradually work on his own and that started to make a real difference. I also went in and did some teaching in his classroom that year, about a two-week unit, where he could see me modify behaviors. That helped him a lot in terms of behavior management and he talked about that. He said that

When staff development failed to yield improvement, principal shifted to frequent conferences.

Conferences began to focus on joint planning.

Principal actually developed plans for the teacher.

Slowly the teacher was weaned from the principal's plans and encouraged to develop his own.

Principal also did model teaching.

seeing me doing it made a difference. So he showed improvement, I would say, though he still had a ways to go. If I were to start over with this particular person, I would be better able to determine what his problems were now than when I started. I also would have more confidence in terms of what I would expect from him. I would not be so hesitant to state my expectations and have him meet them.

Principal feels she was too slow to express her expectations.

Researcher: Is it possible that all the effort simply isn't worth it? Are you salvaging somebody who shouldn't be in the profession in the first place?

Linda: That's a good question. It depends on how you look at who should be in the profession. If you are looking for super competent teachers, then no; but if you are looking for an average person, who we generally have teaching in the schools, then yes. He was capable. I think his problem was motivation with knowledge and skill weaknesses. But, if I had been more skilled, I could have brought him along a lot further. It is very time-consuming to do intensive supervision with teachers who are having a lot of difficulty. Certainly, it is a lot easier to have better ones to begin with. They will pick up a lot of things that you do through staff development and if you do less supervision with lots of feedback, they don't need as much. Although, it is important to do it with them because they enjoy it and really grow quickly.

With bright teachers who learn quickly, staff development may suffice for improvement.

Researcher: Awhile back you mentioned that you used the informal observations to plan individual and group staff development. Is it the case that you would use your observation and diagnosis of them to suggest to them courses they could take on an individual basis?

Linda: Yes. I did that with the one teacher that I mentioned earlier. She loved the course she took and it made a tremendous difference for her. I have suggested classes to other teachers as well, but I tended to rely more on my own teaching to the staff or my own work with the staff rather than recommending they go elsewhere.

Principal both taught her staff and recommended courses they can take.

Researcher: Did you create small groups, subsets of staff, to work on a particular common problem that they had? How did that work?

Linda: Yes. There were problems that were tied to staff development that I did with the whole group. For example, I would present how to do long-range planning to the whole group and then I also would go around and help individual teams, such as the second-grade team, work on long-range planning, relating it specifically to their grade level, group of kids, and teaching styles. So, it was more individualized. Then, if people still had difficulty, I would meet with them on a one-to-one basis. My last year at the school, I got smart enough to ask teachers if they wanted to use their

Principal encouraged teams of teachers to tackle problems and grow together.

Principal allowed teachers to use professional days for intensive supervision with her.

professional days to work with me, one on one all day. I would work with them individually.

Another thing we were trying to do was improve the science program at the school and decide on some basic concepts and skills to teach at each grade level, so that we wouldn't keep doing the same thing over and over. We wanted to develop some units and decide how to teach them alone or in teams. So I would help each team with that. Each team would be different depending on the people, how they wanted to work together, and what their skills were. I did a lot of small group as well as large group work. When a teacher was having trouble or wanted help in a particular area, such as composition, I worked individually. I would have them list areas that they wanted help in, and then I would bring materials to them or sit down and talk with them. One teacher had a lot of trouble with transitions. It took the kids 10–15 minutes to get their books and pencils out. She is going crazy, but she couldn't figure out what to do about it. In those instances, I didn't always help the teacher, but hooked them up with another teacher to help them. There was another teacher who handled those kinds of things very well and shared information with that teacher. It changed her life. She was really grateful. It just took a few minutes, but it made a big difference.

Researcher: Would you classify her as a more competent teacher than the first two teachers you talked about?

Principal worked with small groups of faculty members on curriculum project.

Teachers were encouraged to share tips with each other.

Linda: Yes, but she was different. She was weak in relation to the style of teaching that I felt worked more effectively with a particular group of students. She was less able to target instruction. For example, she did a lot of interesting things with kids, but they lacked focus and she had a lot of difficulty with planning. It took her hours and hours to do and it was difficult for her to focus on skills and organize activities. So I had to work with her, but in terms of a casual observation, things were going fine.

Researcher: Let's go to the other end of the continuum, specifically, teachers who you regard as outstanding. Can you think of a highly skilled teacher who you were able to help also?

Linda: They're not as dramatic, but those kinds of things came out of those general and formal conferences. One excellent teacher tended to overshoot the capabilities of her kids. She was really good and she would eventually get them there, but she tended to teach a little bit over their heads. So, when I made observations in her classroom, I pointed those kinds of things out to her and the children who were having difficulty. I talked with her about how to address things.

Outstanding teachers can grow, too.

Researcher: Was it sufficient for you to simply point out the problem and was she able to adjust?

Linda: I had to keep pointing it out.

Researcher: Did you point it out and suggest strategies?

Linda: Yes. I talked to her about it. With those better teachers, as with all the teachers, I would look at the work the kids were doing. When you are working with higher-achieving teachers, who pick up right away, all you have to do is mention ideas and they get other ideas. What you can do best with them is to share and brainstorm, give them initial guidance and direction. Of course, I also have a lot of instructional resource materials that I share with the teachers.

Or, if they were planning a unit, I helped write units for teachers. I wrote units as models. If they needed it, I would write one to show them how to put one together. Then they would use it and get ideas off it. My higher-achieving teachers would look at something like that and they would come up with 300 better ideas on their own. I had a group of teachers of second grade who had a lot of difficulty due to lack of motivation or whatever putting together science units. Rather than hassle them about it, I wrote one for them and had them implement it. Then they started feeling comfortable with it. They got more ideas and went about doing more on their own. I offered support to whatever level I needed to make a step forward and if that meant writing a unit and having them do it, I did that. If it meant sitting down with them for a whole day and planning together, that is what I would do.

The focus of principal's interactions with teachers tended to be students and their work or behavior.

Principal shared resource materials with teachers.

Principal was always willing to model and demonstrate.

Principal never gave up on a teacher.

Researcher: As you planned the general staff development activities for everyone, would you plan them more around what you thought to be the needs of teachers based on your observations of them or more on what you happened to regard as priorities for that year?

Linda: Initially, I planned them based on what I thought good instruction should be and where I saw teachers in relation to that.

Principal had a clear vision of effective instruction to guide her in her work with teachers.

Researcher: One of the difficulties in delivering good staff development is teacher turnover. You work with somebody for a year and then they're gone. So you have to deal with the induction of a new person and bringing them up to speed. Did you have much turnover in your staff?

Linda: No, I didn't. When I had a new person coming in who needed help in something that the staff was already pretty competent in, I would put him with one of my better staff members and have them teach the new person.

Principal paired new teachers with experienced veterans to facilitate induction.

Researcher: You mentioned before how much time it took. Is it unreasonable to expect everyone in administration to have your level of expertise and inexhaustible energy. What is reasonable to expect? What would you do if you were to start over again?

Linda: If I were starting over again, I would have a much better sense of

what staff development needs were
and what I needed to teach and a better sense of how to pace staff development activities. I thought I did a good
job on follow up, but I see now that I
really could have done better. I could
have paced it slower, presented more
concrete examples to people. I should
have given people more opportunities
to practice where I could watch them
and give them more help. So, I would
be a little more systematic. I think the
more you learn in curriculum and instruction, the more you are able to be
efficient. With that teacher recently, I
was able to address a really major
problem fast and, at least for the week
following that conference, it made a
big difference in what he was able to
do. I don't know if I would have been
able to do that four years ago.

Principal is aware she may have tried to do too much too quickly.

Principal is always improving her own supervisory skills.

Researcher: Let's address the role of
student achievement data in evaluation. Did you feel that you needed the
test data to justify what you were going to do in evaluation and supervision? Did you need the statistics to
back you up when you went in and
said, "Look, you need changes here?"

Linda: Yes, that was helpful to me. It
was something concrete to work on.
Without test data, you can never get a
fix on the problem. Now, I could help
get a fix through observations much
more quickly and better than I was
able to before, but it helps to have
some kind of objective data.

Test scores helped guide the principal in her improvement efforts with teachers.

Researcher: What do you mean by *objective?*

Linda: The district tests. The test scores show that you have a child performing below standards. We gave the Stanford Diagnostic Test in Reading and I had that to look at.

Researcher: Was it ever the case that the teacher's own assessment information created a need for growth in some particular area? Might there be evidence that exists as a result of in-class assessment?

Linda: Definitely. Areas that we focused on did not all come from me. They often came from the teachers. The longer I stayed there, the more they came from the teachers.

Teachers also were able to determine the agenda for improvement.

Researcher: Based in part on the teachers assessment of student achievement, not standardized assessment?

Linda: Yes. That was always a part of our evaluation. You know you don't have enough information on them. But what we hoped to get was more specific and precise information from teachers' observations rather than vague, "Gee, he really can't read." Teachers make statements like that. I tried to get people to be more specific, "What do you mean?" so that we could start to address them. As we focused on skills, they were able to identify those skills and make observations where they could identify the particular skills kids were having trouble with.

Supervisor encouraged teachers to achieve greater precision in describing student problems. Primary thrust in supervision was how to help individual students, not how to correct teacher deficiencies.

Researcher: What do you accept as evidence that the growth has taken place? Is it a feeling? Do you look at the kid's performance?

Linda: I look at how the kids behave. I look at the change in their performance and whether they are learning to read or write, how their writing is changing, what their interests are. Are they interested in what they are doing; are they happy? I ask them how they feel about the school. Teachers would talk about how much they learn. Former teachers say, "We miss having someone come in to observe us who really knows what we are doing."

The credibility of the principal is linked to her familiarity with what goes on in each teacher's classroom.

Researcher: How can we improve this communication?

Linda: I don't think administrators know what to tell the teacher.

I am involved in administrative training this year, so that is an issue that comes to mind every day. I think it is quite possible for a large number of administrators to be much improved in terms of their instructional leadership skills. I think one of the biggest battles you fight with administrators is the motivation to get down to business and learn the curriculum in at least one major area all the way through school. Language arts is one area that goes in every subject area. If you are going to choose one area you want people to be skilled in, that's probably the more important one because it is generalized. The expectation for principals to do that is very

Supervisors need training in instructional leadership.

Principals need to understand the curriculum as it cuts across grade levels.

Expectations for supervisors need to be

important because if they aren't motivated internally to do that, someone else is going to have to motivate them. It is just like teachers in a building doing an average job and feeling okay about themselves and geting along with others but then they aren't doing anywhere near the job of teaching that they could. Administrators do the same thing. The expectation level has to be there at the district level. "We expect you to be instructional leaders. We will give you the training you need to do that." The motivation will come to these people after they become involved in these activities. It is very rewarding. If you are able to manage a school and you don't get bored with that, why would you want to take on this other job in instructional leadership? I think it is fun. It is the only reason I became a principal. I wanted some control. There is still a lot of talk about instructional leadership but I don't think the expectation is really there. I am interested and motivated. I talk to teachers if I don't know something and can learn from them.

higher if we are to encourage instructional leadership.

Principal was open to learning from teachers.

Researcher: Thank you for your thoughts.

FOUR

Analysis and Summary
of Effective Cases*

These cases represent but a few of the many we studied in which a high-quality teacher evaluation triggered teacher improvement. These particular cases were selected for inclusion here because they illustrate many of the factors that appear important in promoting productive evaluation. Space will not permit us to provide specific information on all cases. However, through an analysis of the content of the various cases, we were able to identify a wide variety of common attributes. These attributes are listed and discussed. Because our analysis was conceptual rather than scientific and based on a limited number of volunteer cases, we do not argue that the key features we have identified are generalizable to all teachers, supervisors, or evaluations. That is, because of the complexity of human relations in the evaluation context, we cannot predict with certainty which evaluations will or will not be helpful to teachers. However, we do feel that the probability a teacher will benefit from an evaluation increases as the number of these attributes present in that evaluation increases.

---

*The attributes of sound evaluation events were originally published in Duke, D. L. and Stiggins, R. J. *Teacher evaluation: Five Keys to Growth*, Copyright 1986, American Association of Elementary School Principals, American Association of Secondary School Principals and the National Education Association, Washington D.C. This adaptation of the original material is included by permission.

Keys to Effective Evaluation

At least five factors contribute to the quality and impact of any particular teacher evaluation experience. These will first be identified and then discussed in detail. Key factors include the people who participate in the evaluation and the manner and environment in which they interact. Participants in the process are the *teacher* and the *evaluator(s)*. Teachers vary in competence, interpersonal manner, knowledge, and experience. They also vary in their perceptions of the evaluator(s). Similarly, those who observe and evaluate teachers—including principals, department heads, other teachers, and students—all bring different viewpoints, temperaments, skills, knowledge, and experience to the process. Based on our case studies, we know that both teachers and evaluators bring to the evaluation experience attributes that are keys to teachers' growth.

The impact of an evaluation also is dictated to a great extent by two key dimensions of the evaluation process: the nature and quality of the evaluation *procedures* used, and the nature and quality of the *feedback* provided to the teachers. For example, procedures can vary in the clarity with which they spell out performance standards or criteria. Performance data can be gathered formally or informally, with varying degrees of frequency and depth of information by a variety of different evaluators. Feedback provided to teachers can vary in amount, frequency, and quality—each difference potentially altering the impact of evaluation.

And finally, the teacher, evaluator(s), procedures, and feedback all come together within a particular *context* for any specific teacher, and contexts can vary greatly. Several factors can cause variations in evaluation systems: differences in the resources available for evaluation and professional development; and differences in district values and policies regarding the purposes and variations in methods used for evaluation. Our cases reveal certain characteristics of contexts that promote growth-oriented teacher evaluation.

Therefore, we regard the five keys to success in teacher evaluation to be the teacher, the evaluator(s), the procedures, the feedback, and the context. Let's explore each in depth.

Important Attributes of the Teacher

The case studies make it clear that one critical factor in the success of a teacher evaluation is the teacher. Like adults in general, teachers go through various stages of development. They reflect individual interests, abilities, values, beliefs, and experiences. There is little reason to expect these characteristics to remain constant over time. A probationary teacher is apt to deal with the evaluation process differently than a tenured teacher. A talented veteran will not react the same as a teacher having difficulty.

At least six teacher attributes emerge from the case studies as possible influences on the outcomes of the evaluation process.

Instructional Competence

The teachers studied by and large were very competent. They would not be identified as teachers who "need" to correct deficiencies, in an accountability sense. They were skilled professionals whose skills grew as a result of the events they described. Since much of the evaluation process focuses on the delivery of instructional services in classrooms, what a teacher knows and thinks he or she knows can help determine the quality of the evaluation experience. Given constructive feedback on the need to alter practice, the teacher who is aware of the options available is more likely to change in a desirable direction.

Since research continuously is providing new insights regarding effective instructional practice, teachers are obliged to remain current in their profession. Teachers who are willing and able to keep abreast of new developments in instructional design, evaluation, or classroom management, for example, are those who are most likely to grow from a solid evaluation experience.

Personal Expectations

The teachers we studied—teachers who grew as a result of evaluation—tended to expect a great deal of themselves. Teachers vary on this scale. Some teachers expect to be effective with all students. Others reason that it is impossible to succeed with everyone. Some teachers expect to keep reading and learning about their field. Others assume that a point is reached where they have mastered their profession. It is likely that teachers who demand a great deal of themselves will benefit most from the evaluation process.

Openness to Suggestion

Personal expectations are closely related to a teacher's openness to constructive suggestions. Growth will occur more quickly when teachers acknowledge the value of feedback from others. The case studies suggested that useful information can be provided by a variety of people, including supervisors, fellow teachers, students, specialists, parents, teacher educators, and researchers. Teachers who benefit most from insights derived from these data sources are those who are open to suggestions that might enhance their effectiveness.

Orientation to Change

Professions like teaching are too complex ever to be mastered fully. There are new techniques to learn and new ideas to test. When one approach fails to work well, teachers can speculate on the reasons, select an alternative approach, and try it out. Effective teaching is a matter of constant experimentation and calculated risk taking. Teachers in the case studies tended to be open to such change. A variety of reasons explain why these individuals welcomed new opportunities: expectation of success if they try something new; a need for success; the teacher's amount of commitment; the perceived presence of support during the change process; and the reservoir of ideas from themselves and others about how to change.

Subject Knowledge

Technical knowledge of instruction is one thing; content knowledge is quite another. Content knowledge consists of two elements: knowledge of the subject matter area in general and knowledge of the district's curriculum plan. The teachers we studied were very well informed about the content they taught.

How much a teacher knows about his or her subject can exert a great influence on the impact of the evaluation process.

Experience

In addition to a teacher's experience with a particular subject or content area, the individual's general professional experience is likely to play a major role in how he or she deals with evaluation. Among the experiences that influenced the responsiveness to evaluation of our case study teachers were the following: record of success with students; reputation for classroom control; previous evaluations and relationships with supervisors; reactions from parents and peers; and seniority in the school and district.

Teachers with a history of useful evaluations are more likely to benefit from future evaluations than those for whom the process has been uninspiring and uninformative. In other instances, the impact of experience is not as easily predicted. For example, teachers with a history of success with students may have the confidence and ego-strength to permit them to take full advantage of the evaluation process.

Important Attributes of the Person Who Observes and Evaluates

Supervisors, like teachers, bring different attributes to the process. Ideally, it would be possible to provide every teacher with a supervisor perfectly matched to his or her needs and interests. Since this kind of matching is unlikely, it makes sense to identify those general characteristics of supervisors that most teachers acknowledge as vital to the success of the evaluation process.

At least six attributes of the supervisor that may affect the quality of the teacher evaluation experience emerged from our case studies.

Credibility

It is difficult to imagine a teacher taking evaluation seriously when the evaluator is perceived to possess little valuable knowledge of direct relevance to teachers, their content area, grade level, or particular group of students.

The supervisors of the teachers we studied all established themselves as credible sources of information for the teachers they supervised. This credibility was established through direct professional contact and careful interpersonal communication. That communication revealed to the teacher many of the attributes that will be listed: persuasiveness, patience, trustworthiness, etc. But more to the point, it included facts and ideas that informed the teacher about the supervisor's knowledge of the technical aspects of teaching, subject matter knowledge, experience in the classroom, and familiarity with the teacher's class and situation.

Persuasiveness

Credibility may be important for teacher growth, but it is insufficient alone. Our case studies also suggest that the evaluator must be able to persuade teachers to alter their actions by providing clear, convincing reasons why change is needed. The teachers we talked with changed because they were convinced that change was necessary. The rationale were persuasive.

Another challenge the supervisor may face is that of convincing the teacher that trying a new instructional approach—experimenting in order to improve—is not only acceptable but is a sign of good teaching. Persuasiveness is required in this context because evaluation has become synonymous with personnel action for most teachers. When someone feels his or her job may be on the line, risk taking is not likely to be the highest priority. The effective evaluator lets teachers know when their jobs are not in jeopardy and allows them the freedom to experiment and grow. This occurred in the cases we studied.

Patience

Supervisors typically have more to do than time available to do it. Cutting corners is always a temptation. There is no substitute, however, for patience in the evaluation process. It may be easier to justify the time required to do evaluation well when it is realized that (a) few activities in which supervisors engage have as great a potential impact, and (b) a great deal of time can be wasted correcting the mistakes resulting from poor evaluations. Time also is required to support teachers as they react to evaluation data, draw their own inferences, respond to evaluators' analyses, and speculate on growth strategies. Supervisors in the case studies were willing to give teachers time and space to reflect on the feedback they provided. Knowing when to back off, when to involve others in the observation and evaluation process, and when to press an issue with a teacher is crucial.

Trust

The ability to inspire trust is important for those who would presume to suggest changes in teacher behavior. Those who can inspire trust, as did supervisors of the teachers we studied, are able to deliver even the most critical feedback without jeopardizing their relationship with teachers.

The case studies suggest that trust may be related to some of the following:

- Supervisors' intentions (what they and the teacher regard as the ultimate purpose of evaluation)
- Maintaining confidentiality in communication
- How a supervisor handles evidence of performance from sources other than the classroom (e.g., hearsay and complaints)
- The consistency with which the supervisor applies evaluation rules and regulations
- The extent to which the teacher and the supervisor see themselves as partners in the school improvement effort
- The honesty and sincerity of interpersonal communications
- The extent to which the teacher has an opportunity to interpret evaluation data first before sharing it with others
- The extent to which teachers participate in the selection of performance goals.

Track Record

Every supervisor acquires a track record. In other words, their observations and advice are judged in light of subsequent events. If teachers discover, for instance, that "sure-fire solutions" made by a supervisor really "work," they are more likely to take the supervisor seriously. Many teachers we interviewed listened to suggestions given, because the giver had established a reputation for being helpful.

Modeling

One of the most effective ways for an observer to make a suggestion is to demonstrate a new idea or technique. This is one reason peers can make excellent evaluators. Teachers then have the opportunity to see what the recommendation looks like in practice. Although modeling under simulated conditions can be effective, an impact is most profound when the recommended practice is performed in the teacher's own classroom. Many of the supervisors in the case studies modeled good practice for the teachers with whom they worked.

Important Attributes of the Procedures Used to Gather Data on Teacher Performance

The growth our teachers experienced was influenced by the quality and perceived usefulness of the feedback they received. Feedback is only as helpful as the quality of the data gathered on the performance of any particular teacher. The quality of the data is determined, in turn, by the appropriateness of the procedures used to gather it.

The procedural profile of any particular evaluation comprises three basic elements: the manner in which issues of performance standards or criteria are addressed; the various information sources tapped to evaluate performance; and the procedures used to gather information on classroom performance. Each element can contribute significantly to the quality and impact of the evaluation.

Performance Criteria and Standards

Performance criteria define the dimensions of teacher performance to be evaluated. Performance standards represent levels of performance required with respect to the criteria. In our case studies, we found that those criteria and standards must be given careful consideration prior to any evaluation They must focus clearly on important aspects of the teaching/learning process, be objectively observable, and be communicated clearly to the teacher. In our studies, the case studies revealed that growth-producing evaluations tend to be based on criteria and standards that are appropriate for the individual context and capabilities of each teacher; endorsed by the teachers as important for them; and informative about the degree to which each teacher's professional goals have been attained.

Data Collection Procedures

The performance data gathered in any particular evaluation can vary because of the source of the data and the manner in which it is collected. For example, in the cases we studied, evidence of teacher performance was derived from observations of teachers' actual classroom performance, the examination of classroom and school records (e.g., lesson plans, etc.), and the examination of student achievement. Any one used alone may be insufficient because it may fail to provide a complete picture of how the teacher (a) prepares for, (b) presents, and (c) evaluates the impact of instruction. Reliance on multiple sources of performance information may be wise if the goal is teacher growth.

When classroom observations are used, our studies revealed, they can take many forms. They can be formal in the sense that they are planned and are preceded and followed by a conference between the supervisor and teacher. Or, they can be informal, as in the case of unannounced drop-in visits. They also can vary in frequency, ranging from one or two formal visits per year to almost daily informal drop-in visits. And finally, observations can vary in length from a few moments to an entire class period and more.

But what degree of formality, frequency, and length is most appropriate for promoting growth? The answer appears to vary greatly from teacher to teacher, school to school, and as a function of the teacher's professional development goal. However, some generalizations seem warranted. The goal of observation is to obtain a representative sample of teacher performance from which to draw conclusions about a teacher's general performance. It is often difficult to draw confident generalizations from a sample of only one or two brief observations. An ongoing sequence of regular visits and discussions is optimal if time permits.

What should observers look for? Teachers in the case studies expressed a preference for descriptive (i.e., nonjudgmental) data. Evaluating this descriptive information is not carried out until later, usually during a postobservation conference. Observers must understand how to use the tools of description. These tools may include narrative description of events as they unfold, strategies for keeping track of particular important student and/or teacher behaviors as they occur (e.g., describing or counting), and videotaping for later debriefing with the teacher, among other things. Sound, growth-producing evaluation begins with an objective record of teacher performance, not with impressionistic or judgmental feedback on the quality of classroom events.

Classroom records represent a valuable source of information from which to derive needed directions for professional development. For example, lesson plans reflect the extent to which teachers have thought through and planned their instructional intentions. Tests, quizzes, assignments, and other assessments may reflect the extent to which teachers have (a) clarified their expectations to students and (b) linked assessment to instruction. Teachers' grading practices and comments on returned papers reveal key dimensions of student performance valued by the teacher. Student notes may reveal which instruction worked and which needs to be reworked. The teachers in our case studies indicated that a variety of such data have played a role in their evaluation experiences.

A Comment on the "Evaluator"

It is convenient and perhaps traditional to think of the teacher's evaluator as being the teacher's supervisor. For the elementary teachers we studied, this was the principal. For the secondary teachers, often it was the principal, assistant principal, or department head. When the purpose of the evaluation is accountability, it is often required by law and contract that the supervisor and evaluator be the same. However, when the goal is to promote teacher growth and development, the case studies suggest a variety of resource people may have contributions to make. While a teacher's self-assessment may be considered self-serving and, therefore, inadmissable in an accountability evaluation, that teacher's own perspective on an aspect of personal growth can be invaluable to professional development. Evaluation by a colleague may be challenged in an adversarial battle with the teacher's association over dismissal of one of its members, but there may be no more qualified source of growth-oriented feedback on teacher performance than another experienced, competent teacher. Teachers' take their colleagues' views to heart and learn from them. Student evaluations of teacher performance might be suspect when a teacher's job is at stake, but there may be no more valid source of information on and criticism of learning environments than the students who live and work in those environments. When their views are sought in a careful, thoughtful way, students can provide insights no one else can.

In short, if we think of only one set of evaluation procedures to be applied rigidly to all teachers and if we allow strict legal constraints to dictate those procedures, we eliminate from our repertoire many of the resources most qualified to trigger and support teacher growth.

Important Attributes of the Feedback

A crucial interpersonal link between the teacher and the observer occurs when the teacher is provided with information on his or her performance. If growth is to occur, it is most likely to begin with this communication, as it did in our case studies. Successful evaluation for whatever purpose requires that feedback procedures be planned and executed carefully. Even the most appropriate information based on the highest quality data collection procedures will go unheeded if not delivered in a sensitive, caring manner. Teachers also appreciate feedback more if it is shared in a private setting, preferably one that represents a "neutral turf."

The case studies suggest that many factors must be considered in planning and delivering feedback on teacher performance. For instance, consider these factors:

- The amount of feedback given at one time—too much can be overwhelming;
- The level of formality needed to achieve desired purposes;
- The way to communicate ideas and suggestions that will make the most sense to the teacher;

- The specificity of the information provided—it must suggest specific actions to the teacher if growth is needed;
- The frequency at which to provide feedback on performance in order to encourage continued development;
- The format to use—whether to convey descriptive information on teacher performance or evaluation judgments regarding that performance;
- The way to time any feedback to ensure maximum impact; and
- The way to be sure the feedback relates to prespecified performance standards.

It is possible to find many teachers annually receiving feedback that reflects general teacher traits as spelled out by state law, but such feedback is unlikely to contribute much to teacher development. The kind of feedback that is apt to encourage growth, our studies reveal, comes from a credible source (or sources), describes specific aspects of their teaching along with ideas and suggestions for improvement that make sense in terms of their contexts, arrives with sufficient regularity to allow them to track their improvement, and is as often informal as formal.

Important Attributes of the Evaluation Context

Key ingredients of effective evaluation, as discussed up to this point, include a teacher, an evaluator, data collection procedures, and feedback. While these elements are central and were the focus of most of our discussions with teachers during our case studies, the studies indicate that context also is important. Every school and district boasts its own unique culture: norms, expectations, traditions, and the like. It is impossible to understand fully how the teacher evaluation process functions without knowing something about the setting in which it takes place. Three contextual factors seemed to influence teacher growth based on our case studies.

History of Labor Relations

In contexts where labor-management relations have been strained or evaluation practices have been uneven, employees may be skeptical about and unreceptive to the evaluation process.

One way to minimize these disruptions is to develop evaluation systems in a context where teachers and district administrators are full partners in designing and monitoring the evaluation process, as they were in our case studies. If teachers have a role in determining performance standards, selecting target concerns for observations, and identifying resources for professional development, the system is more likely to result in an evaluation process that is perceived to be helpful and teachers who are more likely to feel a sense of ownership in the system.

Time Spent on Evaluation

Sound evaluation practice requires time. Time is needed for such activities as designing and setting up an evaluation system; convening goal-setting conferences; conducting preobservation conferences; carrying out classroom observations; conducting postobservation conferences; carrying out informal classroom visits and feedback sessions; coordinating the involvement of teachers, students, and others; and individualizing professional development, as in the case of setting up demonstration lessons or arranging visits to other schools.

Where evaluation is not regarded as a high priority, supervisors may begin to take shortcuts. The teachers we interviewed, for example, told of supervisors who skip goal-setting conferences or who have teachers write their own annual evaluations. Many supervisors fall into the habit of leaving a copy of their observations in the teacher's mailbox rather than meeting with the teacher to discuss the visit. Each shortcut increases the likelihood that teachers will not take the evaluation process seriously and, consequently, not derive maximum benefit from it.

Resources Available for Growth

In evaluations that contributed to the professional growth of teachers, resources for development were available. Resources mentioned as important in the case studies included the following:

- Released time for visiting other classrooms, modeling a particular teaching process in a colleague's classroom, attending workshops, etc.;

- Technical assistance from consultants and in-district experts;
- In-class information retrieval systems that allow teachers to gain regular feedback on performance;
- Videotape equipment (with the understanding that videotapes remain in the teacher's possession and release of tapes for viewing by others is up to the teacher);
- Staff development activities (often provided for individual teachers);
- Professional library materials; and
- Peer mentors.

By making resources available to teachers, a district demonstrates to teachers the district's commitment to growth-oriented evaluation.

Summary and Conclusions

Our first series of case studies, which focused on district evaluation systems (Chapter Two), revealed some of the barriers that prevent teacher evaluation from promoting teacher improvement. In addition, the results also suggested actions that might be taken to deal with those barriers. The second set of case studies, described in the preceding chapter and summarized above, provided concrete and heartening evidence that those barriers can be removed. While we found instances of teacher growth resulting from evaluations to be rare, we could find enough instances of success to warrant the conclusion that teachers can benefit from effective evaluation. The key to success, based on our limited number of cases, appears to be careful attention to *all* of the active ingredients in the evaluation process: teachers and supervisors must be willing to contribute to that success; procedures for gathering performance data must be carefully planned and carried out; feedback must be delivered in a thoughtful manner; and the context must be one in which teacher growth is valued. In our third and final study, described in the next chapter, we validate these conclusions.

FIVE

Exploring the Range of Evaluation Experiences

The key attributes described in the last chapter were identified through a content analysis of a limited number of volunteer cases. Consequently, the generalizability of these attributes to other teachers and their experiences remained in question. To address this issue, we examined the recent evaluation experiences of a much larger sample of teachers. Our goal was to validate the list of key attributes of teacher evaluation by determining if these attributes indeed were related to perceived growth outcomes of evaluation. To achieve this goal, we developed the Teacher Evaluation Profile, or TEP, a questionnaire that asked teachers to describe their most recent evaluation, rate its overall quality, and describe its effects on them. Responses to the questionnaire allowed us to explore (a) the relationships among components of the evaluation process, and (b) the relationship between key attributes and various perceived outcomes of the evaluation. In addition, this process produced an instrument that school districts can use to assess the extent to which teacher evaluation is perceived as producing growth.

Research Methodology

Instrument Design

The TEP questionnaire asks teachers to describe their last evaluation in terms of each of the five categories of key attributes described in the previous chapter (see questionnaire in Appendix A). Instructions requested that teachers describe the following factors in each category (Underlined terms henceforth will be used as brief labels for items):

The attributes that they brought to the evaluation event—

1. Their overall competence as a teacher, from minimally competent to outstanding teachers.
2. The strength of their professional expectations of self, from demand little to demand a great deal.
3. Their willingness to take risks.
4. Their interpersonal orientation, from reserved / private to open / public.
5. Attributions of the reasons for their success or failure, assigning responsibility to themselves or others.
6. Their orientation to change, from flexible to slow to change.
7. Their willingness to experiment in the classroom.
8. Their openness to criticism.
9. Their knowledge of technical aspects of teaching.
10. Their knowledge of subject matter.
11. Their teaching experience at current grade level.
12. Their teaching experience with current content.
13. The helpfulness of teacher evaluation prior to your most recent experience.

Their perceptions of the person who evaluated their performance—

14. Evaluator's credibility as a source of feedback.
15. Evaluator's working relationship with teacher, from helper to adversary.
16. Evaluator's level of trust, from trustworthy to not trustworthy.
17. Evaluator's interpersonal manner, from threatening to not threatening.
18. Evaluator's patience.
19. Evaluator's flexibility.
20. Evaluator's knowledge of the technical aspects of teaching.
21. Evaluator's capacity to demonstrate or model needed improvements.
22. Evaluator's familiarity with their classroom.

23. Evaluator's experience in classrooms in general.
24. Usefulness of suggestions for improvement.
25. Persuasiveness of rationale for suggested changes.

The attributes of the evaluation procedures—

26. The manner in which standards were communicated.
27. The clarity of standards.
28. Whether standards were endorsed by them as appropriate for their classroom.
29. The form of the standards (goals or professional traits).
30. The standards unique to that teacher or uniform across teachers.
31. Information from observation of their performance.
32. Information from examination of class or school records.
33. Information from examination of student achievement.
34. The number of formal classroom observations.
35. The number of informal classroom observations.
36. The length of formal observations.
37. The length of informal observations.
38. The number of persons observing and evaluating performance.

Attributes of the feedback—

39. Amount of information received.
40. Frequency of formal feedback.
41. Frequency of informal feedback.
42. Depth of information provided.
43. Quality of ideas contained in feedback.
44. Specificity of information provided.
45. Judgmental or descriptive nature of information provided.
46. Appropriateness of timing of feedback.
47. Extent to which feedback focused on district standards.

Attributes of the context within which the evaluation took place—

48. Amount of time spent by all involved in the evaluation.
49. Amount of time allocated during the teaching day for professional development.

50. Available training programs, from none to many.
51. Clarity of district policy statements regarding the purposes for evaluation.
52. Intended role for evaluation, from teacher accountability to teacher growth.
53. Recent history of labor relations in the district, from turbulent to tranquil.
54. Extent of impact of collective bargaining on evaluation.
55. Extent of impact of state law on evaluation.

In addition to these fifty-five attributes, teachers were also asked to rate the outcome of their last evaluation. Taking into account the entire evaluation process, including planning for evaluation, classroom observations, and feedback, they were asked to rate the *overall quality* of the evaluation on a scale from 0 to 9, with 0 representing poor quality and 9 higher quality.

Next, they were asked to rate the *impact* of that evaluation on three specific aspects of their professional practices. Once again, the rating was on a scale of 0 to 9, with 0 meaning no impact and 9 meaning strong impact. The aspects were

- The *impact on their attitudes* about teaching: A strong impact rating of (9) would reflect a profound change in how they felt about the content they taught, their students, and/ or themselves as teachers.
- The *impact on their teaching behaviors and strategies:* A strong impact (9) would reflect major changes in their instructional behavior, classroom management strategies, evaluation practices, and/or other observable dimensions of their teaching.
- The *impact on their understanding of the teaching/learning process:* A strong impact (9) would reflect a change in their ability to account for effectiveness (or lack thereof), explaining the reasons for instructional decisions, and/or a better understanding of student needs or behavior.

Participating Teachers

The TEP was completed by 470 teachers from five school districts. In four of the five districts, every teacher in the district participated. These represented 416 of the total sample. The remainder were on staff in a district of over 1000 teachers. One hundred teachers were selected at random to respond; fifty-four did so.

Districts participated on a voluntary basis because of administrators' interest in examining their teacher evaluation systems. Three of the five districts were suburban; two were rural. Four were located in Oregon; one was an island jurisdiction in the western Pacific Ocean. Districts were not selected to represent any particular array or population of districts or teachers. Therefore, generalization beyond this sample should be made with great caution.

Questionnaires were distributed to teachers, collected, and returned to the researchers by district personnel. Data were collected in the fall of the 1986–87 academic year.

Data Analyses

Teachers' responses were analyzed in three phases. The first sought information related to the dependability of the original structure of items built into the questionnaire. Coefficient alphas were computed to estimate the internal consistency reliability of items within each of the five scales or categories of attributes. In addition, Pearson product-moment correlation coefficients were used to examine relationships among the five scale scores. Scale scores were defined as the mean response to all items within the scale. In addition, item intercorrelations were examined using principle components factor analysis. Varimax rotation of the fifty-five item correlation matrix were used to examine four-, five-, and six-factor solutions.

The second phase of the analysis focused on relationships between attributes of the evaluation and the outcome of the event as seen by the teacher. The purpose was to explore the relative importance of various attributes in determining the outcomes of evaluation. First, correlations were computed between and among the four outcomes rated by teachers: overall quality and impact on attitudes, behavior, and understanding. Then the relationship was explored between each of the fifty-five questionnaire items and the four outcome ratings. This was done in two ways. First, the complete 4×55 correlation matrix was generated and subsequently a stepwise regression analysis was conducted with individual questionnaire items as predictor variables and outcome ratings as criteria.

Phase two also included an examination of the predictive efficiency of scale scores using outcome ratings as criteria. Two regression analyses were carried out: one identified five scale scores as the mean response to items within each of the original five categories of attributes; and the other defined scale scores as factor scores in which item responses were weighted according to factor loadings in the four-factor solution varimax rotation.

The third and final phase of the analysis addressed issues related to the sensitivity of the questionnaire to differences in evaluations across the five districts. One analysis focused on consistency in correlations between questionnaire items and outcome ratings across districts. Complete 4×55 correlation matrices were generated for each district with items as predictors and outcome ratings as criteria. In addition, a multivariate analysis of variance was carried out with the school district as the independent variable and the original five scale scores as dependent measures, in order to explore the sensitivities of those scores to differences across districts.

Research Results

The results are presented in accordance with the three phases of the analysis.* Tables 2–9 reveal relationships between and among the fifty-five items tapping attributes of the evaluation event. Tables 10–13 explore relationships between attributes and outcomes of teacher evaluation; and Tables 14–17 examine differences in response patterns across districts.

Relationships Among Questionnaire Items

Table 2 examines two facets of the relationship among questionnaire items. First, internal consistency reliabilities are reported on the diagonal for each of the five scales originally built into the questionnaire. Items within each scale are highly correlated, with *evaluator* and *feedback* scales having the highest internal consistency. It is worthy of note that the internal con-

---

*Means and standard deviations of responses to individual questionnaire items are reported by district in Appendix B.

Table 2

Internal Consistency
Reliability Estimate of and Intercorrelations
Among Original Five Scales (reliabilities on the diagonal)

	(1)	(2)	(3)	(4)	(5)
Attributes of teacher	.72				
Attributes of evaluator	.22	.94			
Attributes of evaluation procedures	.17	.58	.77		
Attributes of feedback	.16	.70	.76	.89	
Attributes of context	.18	.55	.58	.60	.71

sistency reliability of the total fifty-five item instrument was .93, suggesting that the questionnaire asks a highly cohesive set of questions about the evaluation process.

The very high estimate of internal consistency of the total instrument suggests that the scales are both internally consistent and highly correlated. The scale intercorrelations in Table 2 show this to be the case. While the scale related to attributes of the *teacher* appears quite independent of the others, the other four scales are moderately to highly correlated.

To explore the properties of TEP further, we conducted a factor analysis of the fifty-five item correlation matrix using varimax rotation to yield orthogonal factors. We equated four-, five- and six-factor solutions. These are reported in Tables 3, 4, and 5.

Looking first at Table 3, the four-factor varimax solution, we find the first factor loading most heavily on items related to attributes of the evaluator. Certain attributes of the feedback, however, also are important here. The second factor appears to be comprised of items related to evaluation procedures including more aspects of feedback than factor one. The third factor is dominated by teacher-related items, while the final factor con-

The Case for Commitment to Teacher Growth

Table 3

Factor-Loading Matrix for Four-Factor Solution, Varimax Rotation

	Factor 1	Factor 2	Factor 3	Factor 4
Teacher:				
1. Competence			.526	
2. Expectations of Self			.473	
3. Risk Taking			.567	
4. Interpersonal Orientation			.370	
5. Attribution Success/Failure				
6. Orientation to Change			.381	
7. Experiment in Class			.505	
8. Openness to Criticism			.351	
9. Technical Knowledge			.553	
10. Subject Knowledge			.500	.368
11. Experience (Grade)				.616
12. Experience (Content)				.678
13. Experience (Teacher Evaluation)	.406			
Evaluator:				
14. Credibility	.685	.364		
15. Relationship to Teacher	.730			
16. Trustworthiness	.780			
17. Interpersonal Manner	.717			
18. Patience	.693			
19. Flexibility	.719			
20. Technical Knowledge	.653	.311		
21. Capacity to Model	.676	.311		
22. Familiar with Classroom	.556	.373		
23. Experience in Classroom	.623	.305		
24. Useful Suggestions	.692	.420		
25. Persuasive Rationale	.669	.359		
Procedures:				
26. Standards Communicated		.521		
27. Standards Clear	.437	.470		
28. Standards Endorsed	.503			
29. Form of Standards				
30. Standards Unique				
31. Classroom Observation		.517		
32. Examine Records		.554		
33. Examine Achievement		.382		
34. No. of Formal Observations		.522		
35. No. of Informal Observations				
36. Formal Length		.488		
37. Informal Length		.400		
38. No. of Observers				

Table 3 (Cont.)

Factor-Loading Matrix for Four-Factor Solution, Varimax Rotation

	Factor 1	Factor 2	Factor 3	Factor 4
Feedback:				
39. Amount of Information		.653		
40. Frequency Formal		.648		
41. Frequency Informal		.456		
42. Depth of Information	.477	.638		
43. Quality of Ideas	.626	.525		
44. Specificity of Information	.433	.589		
45. Nature of Information	.510	.350		
46. Timing of Feedback	.382	.400		
47. Focused on Standards	.383	.501		
Context:				
48. Time Spent on Evaluation				
49. Time for Professional Development				
50. Training Available				
51. Clear Evaluation Policy	.380	.388		
52. Intended Role	.509			
53. Labor Relations				
54. Collective Bargaining Impact				
55. State Law Impact		.333		
Percent of Variance	24.2	4.9	4.1	2.7

tains just three items—all reflecting years of teaching experience.

In Table 4, the five-factor solution again begins with a strong evaluator/feedback factor followed by a procedures factor including feedback. The second factor loads most heavily on procedures and feedback items, while the third factor has its largest loadings on three feedback items. Meanwhile, the fourth and fifth factors related to the teacher and teaching experience. All but one of the ingredients of the original structure play a role in this solution.

The six-factor varimax solution, reported in Table 5, also shows the evaluator and feedback factor followed by a procedures and feedback factor. In this case, however, the third factor relates to performance standards. The fourth factor contains teacher items, the fifth contains teaching experience

Table 4

Factor-Loading Matrix for Five-Factor Solution, Varimax Rotation

	Factor 1	Factor 2	Factor 3	Factor 4	Factor 5
Teacher:					
1. Competence				.532	
2. Expectations of Self				.507	
3. Risk Taking				.564	
4. Interpersonal Orientation				.341	
5. Attribution Success/Failure					
6. Orientation to Change				.376	
7. Experiment in Class				.517	
8. Openness to Criticism				.345	
9. Technical Knowledge				.554	
10. Subject Knowledge				.507	.345
11. Experience (Grade)					.692
12. Experience (Content)					.749
13. Experience (Teacher Evaluation)	.415				
Evaluator:					
14. Credibility	.680	.357			
15. Relationship to Teacher	.719				
16. Trustworthiness	.773				
17. Interpersonal Manner	.706				
18. Patience	.693				
19. Flexibility	.732				
20. Technical Knowledge	.655				
21. Capacity to Model	.683				
22. Familiar with Classroom	.579		.313		
23. Experience in Classroom	.642				
24. Useful Suggestions	.712		.312		
25. Persuasive Rationale	.678				
Procedures:					
26. Standards Communicated	.338	.634			
27. Standards Clear	.392	.612			
28. Standards Endorsed	.470	.410			
29. Form of Standards					
30. Standards Unique					
31. Classroom Observation		.499			
32. Examine Records		.404	.396		
33. Examine Achievement	.313		.377		
34. No. of Formal Observations		.385	.348		
35. No. of Informal Observations			.327		
36. Formal Length		.490			
37. Informal Length			.390		
38. No. of Observers					

Table 4 (Cont.)

Factor-Loading Matrix for Five-Factor Solution, Varimax Rotation

	Factor 1	Factor 2	Factor 3	Factor 4	Factor 5
Feedback:					
39. Amount of Information	.386	.582			
40. Frequency Formal		.441	.507		
41. Frequency Informal	.319		.440		
42. Depth of Information	.488	.506	.400		
43. Quality of Ideas	.638	.416	.316		
44. Specificity of Information	.434	.508			
45. Nature of Information	.490	.400			
46. Timing of Feedback	.364	.424			
47. Focused on Standards	.352	.565			
Context:					
48. Time Spent on Evaluation		.454	.336		
49. Time for Professional Development			.381		
50. Training Available			.301		
51. Clear Evaluation Policy	.346	.472			
52. Intended Role	.510				
53. Labor Relations					
54. Collective Bargaining Impact					
55. State Law Impact					
Percent of Variance	24.2	5.0	4.2	2.8	2.0

items, and the sixth consists of one item related to time spent for professional development.

Across the various factor analyses, some items tended not to load on any of the factors, regardless of solution. These included item 5, the teacher's attributions of reasons for success or failure; items 29 and 30, related to the form and uniqueness of performance standards; item 35, number of informal observations; item 38, number of persons observing and evaluating performance; and several items in the context category: 50, availability of training; 53, history of labor relations; 54, impact of collective bargaining; and 55, impact of state law.

In summary with respect to item and scale relationships, there is evidence of the cohesiveness among the items on the questionnaire. The statistical infrastructure of items does not exactly match the five categories built into the instrument.

Table 5

Factor-Loading Matrix for Six-Factor Solution, Varimax Rotation

	Factor 1	Factor 2	Factor 3	Factor 4	Factor 5	Factor 6
Teacher:						
1. Competence				.532		
2. Expectations of Self				.502		
3. Risk Taking				.566		
4. Interpersonal Orientation				.350		
5. Attribution Success/Failure						
6. Orientation to Change				.377		
7. Experiment in Class				.516		
8. Openness to Criticism				.350		
9. Technical Knowledge				.556		
10. Subject Knowledge				.507	.356	
11. Experience (Grade)					.678	
12. Experience (Content)					.768	
13. Experience (Teacher Evaluation)	.400					
Evaluator:						
14. Credibility	.674					
15. Relationship to Teacher	.737					
16. Trustworthiness	.784					
17. Interpersonal Manner	.727					
18. Patience	.713					
19. Flexibility	.736					
20. Technical Knowledge	.631					
21. Capacity to Model	.652					
22. Familiar with Classroom	.550					.311
23. Experience in Classroom	.612					
24. Useful Suggestions	.693	.305				
25. Persuasive Rationale	.661					
Procedures:						
26. Standards Communicated			.670			
27. Standards Clear	.344		.730			
28. Standards Endorsed	.445		.475			
29. Form of Standards						
30. Standards Unique						
31. Classroom Observation		.551				
32. Examine Records		.420				.324
33. Examine Achievement						.342
34. No. of Formal Observations		.524				
35. No. of Informal Observations						.311
36. Formal Length		.554				
37. Informal Length		.382				
38. No. of Observers						

Table 5 (Cont.)

Factor-Loading Matrix for Six-Factor Solution, Varimax Rotation

	Factor 1	Factor 2	Factor 3	Factor 4	Factor 5	Factor 6
Feedback:						
39. Amount of Information	.413	.657				
40. Frequency Formal		.649				
41. Frequency Informal	.319	.437				
42. Depth of Information	.510	.630				
43. Quality of Ideas	.642	.463				
44. Specificity of Information	.438	.516				
45. Nature of Information	.511	.332				
46. Timing of Feedback	.388	.400				
47. Focused on Standards	.355	.400	.400			
Context:						
48. Time Spent on Evaluation		.465				
49. Time for Professional Development						.455
50. Training Available						.367
51. Clear Evaluation Policy	.332		.435			
52. Intended Role	.494					
53. Labor Relations						
54. Collective Bargaining Impact						
55. State Law Impact						
Percent of Variance	24.3	5.0	4.2	2.8	2.1	1.8

With the possible exception of the context factor, though, there is evidence that each of the original categories has an important place in the structure of item responses (see Table 6).

Relationship Between Attributes and Perceived Outcomes

The relationship between attributes of teacher evaluations and how teachers see the outcomes of those events is seen most clearly in the correlation between the fifty-five item responses and the four rated outcomes. The highest of those correlations are reported in Table 7. The only teacher attribute related to outcome rating is the nature of the teacher's prior experience with the evaluation process. This was rated by teachers on a continuum of "waste of time" to "helpful." Also, each of the

Table 6

Factor Labels for Various Solutions

Factor ID	4 Factor	5 Factor	6 Factor
1	Evaluator + Feedback	Evaluator + Feedback	Evaluator + Feedback
2	Procedures + Feedback	Procedures + Feedback	Procedures + Feedback
3	Teacher	Feedback	Standard
4	Experience	Teacher	Teacher
5		Experience	Experience
6			Professional Development
Percent of Variance Accounted for	35.9	38.1	40.1

attributes of the evaluator is correlated with each of the outcome ratings, as are most of the feedback items. Fewer procedures and context items are related to outcomes. Further, the data suggest that items correlated with the overall quality rating also are related to the impact ratings. However, the correlations with overall quality are typically higher.

Based on the Table 7 data, the ten items most highly correlated with overall quality and impact ratings are these:

14.   Perceived credibility of the evaluator (.65)
43.   Quality of ideas contained in the feedback (.59)
42.   Depth of information contained in the feedback (.58)
25.   Persuasiveness of rationale for suggested changes (.58)
24.   Usefulness of suggestions made (.57)
16.   Trustworthiness of the evaluator (.56)
15.   Helper versus adversary relationship of evaluator (.54)
21.   Evaluator's perceived capacity to demonstrate needed changes (.54)

Table 7

Significant Correlations Between Individual Questionnaire Items and Various Outcome Ratings

	Overall Quality	Impact on		
		Attitude	Behavior	Understanding
Teacher:				
1. Competence				
2. Expectations of Self				
3. Risk Taking				
4. Interpersonal Orientation				
5. Attribution Success/Failure				
6. Orientation to Change				
7. Experiment in Class				
8. Openness to Criticism				
9. Technical Knowledge				
10. Subject Knowledge				
11. Experience (Grade)				
12. Experience (Content)				
13. Experience (Teacher Evaluation)	.42	.29	.32	.36
Evaluator:				
14. Credibility	.65	.32	.32	.36
15. Relationship to Teacher	.54	.29	.29	.26
16. Trustworthiness	.56	.32	.30	.30
17. Interpersonal Manner	.40	.24	.22	.21
18. Patience	.35	.25	.23	.20
19. Flexibility	.42	.26	.21	.22
20. Technical Knowledge	.53	.26	.33	.32
21. Capacity to Model	.54	.28	.31	.34
22. Familiar with Classroom	.52	.31	.32	.33
23. Experience in Classroom	.51	.31	.34	.33
24. Useful Suggestions	.57	.37	.42	.46
25. Persuasive Rationale	.58	.33	.37	.38
Procedures:				
26. Standards Communicated	.42			.22
27. Standards Clear	.46			.20
28. Standards Endorsed	.39			
29. Form of Standards				
30. Standards Unique				
31. Classroom Observation	.32			.23
32. Examine Records	.28	.23	.22	.25
33. Examine Achievement	.32		.23	.23
34. No. of Formal Observations	.21			
35. No. of Informal Observations	.20			
36. Formal Length				
37. Informal Length				
38. No. of Observers				

Table 7 (Cont.)

Significant Correlations Between Individual Questionnaire Items and Various Outcome Ratings

	Overall Quality	Impact on		
		Attitude	Behavior	Understanding
Feedback:				
39. Amount of Information	.49	.22	.24	.30
40. Frequency Formal	.39	.24	.24	.30
41. Frequency Informal	.34		.22	.27
42. Depth of Information	.58	.29	.30	.35
43. Quality of Ideas	.59	.32	.32	.37
44. Specificity of Information	.51	.23	.24	.28
45. Nature of Information	.40			
46. Timing of Feedback	.40			
47. Focused on Standards	.40			.20
Context:				
48. Time Spent on Evaluation	.36			.20
49. Time for Professional Development	.21	.25	.24	.29
50. Training Available				
51. Clear Evaluation Policy	.38			
52. Intended Role	.38	.26	.29	.31
53. Labor Relations	.25	.20		
54. Collective Bargaining Impact				
55. State Law Impact				

Note: Data are reported for the 5 individual districts in Appendix C.

20. Perceived technical knowledge of evaluator (.53)

22. Evaluator's familiarity with the teacher's own classroom (.52)

The similarity of these correlations across different types of outcome ratings raised speculation that the outcomes may have a great deal in common. To test this proposition, correlations were computed among the four outcome ratings. The results are seen in the right hand column of Table 8. These data suggest that the three impact ratings are highly correlated with each other, while remaining somewhat independent of the overall quality rating. Further, as Table 8 shows, these relationships are very consistent across the five school districts. For this reason, subsequent analyses of attribute–outcome rela-

Table 8

Criterion Rating Intercorrelations

	District 1	District 2	District 3	District 4	District 5	Total
Overall Quality:						
Attitude	.37	.44	.44	.32	.57	.44
Behavior	.37	.27	.42	.29	.76	.43
Understanding	.22	.40	.43	.13	.69	.45
Attitude:						
Behavior	.72	.80	.76	.78	.89	.80
Understanding	.67	.88	.69	.57	.84	.73
Behavior:						
Understanding	.79	.88	.81	.68	.88	.82

tionships included a combined impact rating defining the mean of the three highly correlated individual impact ratings.

The relationships of attributes to outcomes also were examined via two kinds of regression analysis. The first was similar in focus to the item by outcome correlation analysis (described earlier) in that items were used as predictor variables to find the most efficient explanation of outcome rating variance. The stepwise regression analysis used takes into account item intercorrelations in generating the prediction equation. The results are presented in Table 9. The issue addressed with these data is this: If we wanted to identify those individual items that (a) correlated most highly with the outcomes and, at the same time, were (b) most independent of each other, what items would be identified? That is, if we wanted to change individual attributes of the evaluation to maximize quality and impact ratings, we might have the greatest chance of doing so by starting with items listed in Table 9. The multiple correlations suggest that we can obtain a fairly accurate prediction of overall quality and a less accurate prediction of impact. Note also that the individual items selected to predict overall quality are not the same as those that consistently predict the various impact ratings.

The final look at attribute–outcome relationships used scale scores rather than individual items as predictor variables. The

Table 9

Regression Equations for the Prediction of Various Outcome Ratings from Individual Questionnaire Items for Total Sample

Criterion Variable	Predictor Variables	Beta	Multiple R
Overall Quality Rating	14. Credibility of Evaluator	.26	.74
	42. Depth of Feedback	.18	
	16. Level of Trust in Evaluator	.16	
	25. Persuasiveness of Rationale	.15	
	27. Clarity of Standards	.12	
	48. Time Spent on Evaluation	.12	
	3. Teacher's Willingness to Risk	-.09	
	38. Number of Persons Evaluating	-.09	
Attitude Impact Rating	24. Usefulness of Suggestions	.27	.42
	49. Time for Professional Development	.13	
	13. Prior Experience with Evaluation	.13	
Behavior Impact Rating	24. Usefulness of Suggestions	.35	.44
	13. Prior Experience with Evaluation	.16	
Understanding Impact Rating	24. Usefulness of Suggestions	.34	.50
	13. Time for Professional Development	.17	
	49. Prior Experience with Evaluation	.14	
Combined Impact Rating	24. Usefulness of Suggestions	.34	.50
	13. Time for Professional Development	.16	
	49. Prior Experience with Evaluation	.14	

original five scale scores were used to predict overall quality and combined impact. The results are presented in Table 10. Using the original scales, attributes of the evaluator and feedback combine to provide the most efficient prediction of overall quality, while attributes of the evaluator and context do the most to accurately predict impact. The overall quality is predicted more effectively than the impact rating.

In summary, with respect to attribute–outcome relationships, there is a great deal of evidence to suggest that the attributes covered in the questionnaire are related to the teachers' ratings of the overall quality and impact of an evaluation event. Perceived characteristics of the evaluator and feedback are most important, with procedures and context playing a secondary role. Attributes of the teacher appear unrelated to perceived outcomes of the evaluation. Within these categories of attributes, we have been able to identify specific items that

Table 10

Regression Equations for the Prediction of Outcomes from Various Subscores

Criterion Variable	Predictor Variables	Beta	Multiple R
Overall Quality	Attributes of the Evaluator	.51	.72
Rating	Attributes of the Feedback	.26	
Combined Impact	Attributes of the Evaluator	.38	.46
Rating	Attributes of the Context	.13	

seem important in determining quality and impact of a teacher evaluation event.

Differences by District

The final phase of analysis explored differences in questionnaire responses across the five districts. Reliable differences across districts would suggest that attributes of evaluations vary as a function of context and that the questionnaire is capable of detecting those differences.

First, we explored differences in patterns of correlation between attributes and outcomes as they changed across districts. In Table 11, we report the number of significant correlations* between items and outcome ratings by district. For example, looking first at the outcome rating of overall quality, thirteen items related to attributes of the teacher could have correlated with that outcome. In District 1, none did. In districts 2, 3, and 5, one did. And in district 4, two items were correlated with overall quality. Scanning this table, it becomes apparent that there were some large differences across districts in the strength of relationship between attributes and outcomes. For instance, with the exception of evaluator and feedback under the quality outcome, District 1 showed few significant relationships. On the other hand, District 3 showed significant correlations between various attributes and outcomes throughout the data.

Between-district differences are also reflected in Table 12, in which equations predicting outcome ratings with individual

---

*The actual correlations are presented in Appendix C.

Table 11

Number of Significant Correlations Between Individual Questionnaire Items and Various Outcome Ratings by District

Outcome Rating	Attributes	District				
		1	2	3	4	5
Overall Quality						
	Teacher (13 items)	0	1	1	2	1
	Evaluator (2 items)	9	12	12	12	12
	Procedures (13 items)	1	4	8	5	8
	Feedback (9 items)	4	7	9	8	9
	Context (8 items)	1	4	7	3	5
Attitude						
	Teacher	0	6	1	0	3
	Evaluator	0	6	12	5	4
	Procedures	0	2	4	3	3
	Feedback	1	2	8	1	3
	Context	1	3	4	3	4
Behavior						
	Teacher	1	4	1	1	3
	Evaluator	0	1	12	2	10
	Procedures	0	0	6	0	4
	Feedback	1	0	9	0	6
	Context	0	1	4	3	5
Understanding						
	Teacher	0	2	1	0	2
	Evaluator	0	6	12	1	10
	Procedures	0	2	8	0	4
	Feedback	0	4	9	0	5
	Context	0	2	5	0	5

Note: Actual correlations are in Appendix C.

items are examined. The most predictive combinations vary greatly by district.

Yet a third way to examine district differences is in terms of mean responses to questionnaire items. We explored this issue via one-way multivariate analysis of variance using districts (with five levels) as the independent variable and the five scale scores as dependent measures. The results are reported in Table 13. The significant multivariate F suggests that there were

Table 12

Regression Equations for the Prediction of Various Outcome Ratings from Individual Questionnaire Items by District

Criterion and Predictor Variables	Beta	Multiple R
Overall Quality Rating		
District 1:		
43. Quality of Ideas in Feedback	.67	.91
28. Standards Endorsed by Teacher	.45	
47. Focus of Feedback on Standards	.37	
2. Teacher's Expectations of Self	-.25	
District 2:		
24. Usefulness of Suggestions	.46	.78
42. Depth of Information in Feedback	.43	
34. No. of Formal Observations	-.25	
District 3:		
14. Credibility of Evaluator	.26	.75
25. Persuasiveness of Rationale for Change	.23	
46. Appropriateness of Feedback Timing	.12	
16. Teacher's Level of Trust in Evaluator	.20	
44. Specificity of Information in Feedback	.15	
District 4:		
14. Credibility of Evaluator	.58	.58
District 5:		
14. Credibility of Evaluator	.64	.79
40. Frequency of Formal Feedback	.28	
Combined Impact Rating		
District 1:		
None*		
District 2:		
13. Prior Experience with Evaluation	.35	.48
4. Interpersonal Orientation	.30	
District 3:		
24. Usefulness of Suggestions	.49	.49
District 4:		
None*		
District 5:		
13. Prior Experience with Evaluation	.47	.62
12. Experience with Content	-.32	

*No partial correlation between item and criterion exceeded a significance level of. 05.

Table 13

Results of One-Way Multivariate Analysis of Variance Comparing
Scale Scores Across Districts

	F	df	p
Multivariate (Hotellings)	8.44	24,814	.000
Univariate:			
Teacher Attributes	2.96	4,460	.020
Evaluator Attributes	7.68		.000
Procedures	13.19		.000
Feedback	7.10		.000
Context	4.51		.001

significant differences across districts with regard to the profile
of five scores. Subsequent univariate F tests for individual
scores reveal significant differences across districts on each
individual score. Summary statistics for scores by district are
reported in Table 14. However, for purposes of the analysis at
hand, the exact nature of the differences is unimportant. The
important fact is that the instrument was sensitive enough to
detect these differences.

Table 14

Summary Statistics for Scale Scores Across Districts

| | District | | | | | | | | | | |
| | 1 | | 2 | | 3 | | 4 | | 5 | | Total |
Score	X̄	SD	X̄	SD	X̄	SD	X̄	SD	X̄	SD	X̄	SD
Teacher	3.93	.34	4.13	.39	4.03	.43	4.05	.36	4.18	.46	4.06	.41
Evaluator	3.37	.70	3.75	.84	3.37	.82	3.72	.70	3.93	1.02	3.54	.85
Procedures	3.37	.42	3.39	.56	2.85	.63	3.12	.54	2.94	.92	3.02	.67
Feedback	3.23	.60	3.50	.87	2.97	.84	3.39	.73	3.17	1.09	3.15	.87
Context	2.47	.42	3.06	.69	2.90	.50	2.86	.57	2.82	1.00	2.88	.67

Summary and Conclusions

Two general conclusions can be supported with the evidence presented: (a) The questionnaire provides high-quality information about teachers' perceptions of their evaluation experience; and (b) there is a strong relationship between specific attributes of an evaluation event and the outcomes of that event as perceived by teachers. Both conclusions warrant further discussion.

Performance of the Questionnaire

The estimates of internal consistency of the questionnaire and its subscales, as well as the results of the factor analyses, suggest that the questionnaire asks a highly cohesive set of questions about the teacher evaluation experience. The probable reason for this is that the questions arise out of actual case studies of successful evaluations (as presented in Chapter 3). Study 3 clearly corroborates the Study 2 results, thus providing some evidence of the generalizability of our research results.

Another reason for the cohesiveness of questionnaire responses is the fact that the items ask teachers to describe a specific event (their last evaluation) rather than general impressions of the evaluation process. This gives the instrument a sharp focus, making data useful at a number of levels. First, each item in the questionnaire describes a particular important facet of the evaluation that can be changed if the results of evaluation are judged inappropriate. This makes the instrument particularly helpful to school districts. Second, reliable scale scores can be computed. These scores provide a convenient way to reduce the fifty-five items to a manageable set of scale scores for research purposes. But what combination of items should be used to create those scale scores? The original structure of the questionnaire included five scales: attributes of the teacher, evaluator, procedures, feedback, and context. The data reveal that these have appropriately high reliabilities and are somewhat independent. However, the factor structure studies revealed slightly different results.

Nevertheless, we conclude that the original five scales should be retained for reporting aggregated questionnaire results. We know that the teacher evaluation events include intricately coupled components. General and highly correlated scales, such as those revealed using factor analysis, are to be expected. Still, the original five scales provide a clear and cohesive basis for communicating with educators about the key ingredients in a sound evaluation. Those who are responsible for evaluations understand that the teacher and evaluator bring crucial attributes to the event. Procedures for conducting the evaluation also are crucial, as is the feedback. These, along with context, represent clearly understood parts of the evaluation process that can be reviewed and changed in terms of specific attributes of each. The original five scales scores are as reliable and predictive of outcomes as weighted factor scores and sensitive enough to detect differences across districts, where the questionnaire is intended to be used (see Table 13). For these reasons, we stand by the original five scales.

Before the instrument is used for the evaluation of a district teacher evaluation system or in a research context, however, some changes are needed.* Items that are (a) apparently outside of the cohesive structure of the five-part questionnaire and (b) unrelated to the quality and impact outcomes of evaluation must be eliminated or revised to increase the data collection efficiency of the instrument. Specific items marked for elimination or modification in the revised questionnaire include

1.   Rate overall competence as a teacher
4.   Orientation to others (private versus public)
5.   Attributions of reasons for success/failure
12.   Experience with current content
29.   The form of the standard (goal versus trait)
38.   Number of different persons evaluating performance
53.   Recent history of labor relations
54.   Impact of collective bargaining on evaluation
55.   Impact of state law on evaluation

---

*In subsequent development of the TEP, these changes have been made, a more efficient instrument has been developed and scoring and reporting services have been developed. For further details, contact the Northwest Regional Educational Laboratory, 101 S.W. Main St., Suite 500, Portland, OR 97204.

The Relation of Attributes to Outcomes

The results suggest that we have uncovered key facets of the relationship between attributes of a teacher evaluation and its perceived impact on teachers. First, the data suggest a strong relationship between the two. Second, we can identify both the scale scores and the individual questionnaire items that are highly related to outcome. The items we feel are most crucial to an effective evaluation are listed in Table 15. Attributes of the

Table 15

Questionnaire Items Seen as Central to Teacher Growth Through Effective Evaluation (in order of importance)

1. Teacher believes that the rationale for suggested changes are persuasive (item 25)
2. Teacher perceives suggested improvements are useful (item 24)
3. Feedback effectively communicates high-quality ideas (item 43)
4. Values and policies of the evaluation context reflect a concern for teacher growth versus teacher accountability (item 52)
5. Teacher perceives evaluator as having extensive experience in the classroom in general (item 23)
6. Evaluator is seen as a credible source of feedback (item 14)
7. Teacher has found previous evaluation experience helpful (item 13)
8. Teacher perceives evaluator as familiar with her or his classroom (item 22)
9. Time is allotted during the teaching day for professional development (item 49)
10. Teacher perceives feedback as providing in-depth information (item 42)
11. Teacher perceives evaluator as having the capacity to demonstrate or model needed improvements (item 21)
12. Teacher perceives evaluator as trustworthy (item 16)
13. Teacher perceives relationship with evaluator as a helping one (item 15)
14. Teacher perceives evaluator as knowledgeable about technical aspects of teaching (item 20)
15. Feedback provides specific information (item 44)
16. Teacher receives frequent formal feedback (item 40)
17. Standards of performance are endorsed by teacher as appropriate for his or her classroom (item 28)
18. Teacher receives frequent informal feedback (item 41)
19. Standards of performance communicated to teacher in detail (item 26)
20. Standards of performance are clear to the teacher (item 27)

evaluator and feedback appear to influence perceived impact most heavily. But we hasten to add that specific attributes within other scales have been identified as very important also and that the particular relationship that obtains may vary somewhat from district to district.

Perhaps the most startling finding in our examination of the relationship of attributes to outcomes is the lack of relationship between teachers' perception of the attributes they bring to the evaluation event and their perceptions of the quality and impact of that event. This may be a statistical artifact due to the lack of variation in the teacher attribute item responses. Teachers tend to rate very high their competence, expectations, risk taking, and so on. Thus, the standard deviations of these items were consistently much lower than for the other items in the questionnaire. This lack of variance can reduce the correlation. Such an explanation can be addressed only with the further accumulation and analysis of data that tap the entire range of teacher attributes. Pending such follow-up research, we continue to feel that these original attributes are central to an effective evaluation.

Another intriguing result of our analysis of attribute–outcome relations is the finding that teachers apparently perceive the overall quality of an evaluation to include more than its impact on them. The data suggest that perceived quality and impact are not highly correlated. Impact, whether it involves changes in attitude, behavior, or understanding, seems to be a unified outcome for teachers. The ratings are highly correlated. If one is high, the others will be high as well. A key research question for the future is what other factors do teachers consider in evaluating the overall quality of an evaluation?

A third important finding in the attribute–outcome analysis is the fact that the attributes tapped by the questionnaire are much more highly correlated with overall quality than with impact. We can predict quality ratings with a fairly high degree of accuracy but do not have such a firm handle on the prediction of impact. Since our major goal is to maximize impact, we must continue the search for additional attributes to enhance our ability to predict this outcome.

Conclusion

In Chapters 3 and 4, we examined cases of successful, growth-producing teacher evaluation. Content analysis and synthesis of those cases produced a list of attributes of successful teacher evaluations. The study described in this chapter reinforced the conclusion that many of the important attributes of teacher evaluation indeed have been identified. In addition, this study produced an instrument, the Teacher Evaluation Profile (TEP), capable of assisting local school districts in evaluating their evaluation systems. If the goal is to develop a growth-producing evaluation system, this instrument can suggest which attributes of the system need attention. In fact, three of the five districts that participated in the study to validate the questionnaire have used the data to convert their teacher evaluation systems to growth-producing formats.

In addition to its relevance for local evaluation, the TEP represents a valuable research tool. It can be used in studies exploring specific strategies for changing components of an evaluation system. For instance, if a district conducts an evaluator training program and wishes to monitor changes in teachers' perceptions, the TEP would be quite useful. Researchers interested in exploring differences in evaluation as a function of grade level, geographic region, variation in state law, or other independent variable could do so using the instrument.

In short, as a result of our research, we now have a clearer idea of the active ingredients in growth-producing teacher evaluation and an instrument that can help us learn even more about sound evaluation in the future. In the concluding chapters, we explore the implications of these results.

SIX

Implications for Research
in Teacher Evaluation

Until recently, much of what has been written about teacher evaluation addressed issues related to evaluation as an accountability tool. The three-year sequence of studies described here represents a departure from that trend. However, this does not represent the only such departure. During this period, other researchers also have seen the need to reexamine the basic assumptions and procedures underlying traditional, unproductive systems of evaluation. In this chapter, we describe the findings of some of those researchers, relate them to our own work, and draw implications for future teacher evaluation research and development.

In addition, we explore the strengths and weaknesses of our research methodology, focusing specifically on the Teacher Evaluation Profile questionnaire and its potential value in furthering an understanding of the teacher evaluation process.

Parallel Research Efforts

Among the teacher evaluation research programs that have addressed issues related to the professional development of teachers are the following:

- McLaughlin and Pfeifer (1986), arising out of the Rand Corporation research of the early 1980s (Wise et al., 1984), addressed evaluation issues as they relate to school organization;
- McGreal (1986), based on consultations with hundreds of school districts, described keys to effective evaluation;

- Bridges (1986) addressed issues related to assisting the incompetent teacher;
- Dornbusch and his associates (Roper & Hoffman, 1986) examined the implementation of collegial evaluation systems;
- Natriello and Wilson (1986) explored evaluation processes in the context of studies of organizational improvement of schools; and,
- Stark and Lowther (1984) probed teachers' evaluation preferences.

In our opinion, each of these investigations provides important insights into the evaluation process and helps us to understand and explain the research results reported in earlier chapters.

For example, McLaughlin and Pfeifer (1986) identify important elements of effective evaluation in four case studies of highly regarded and apparently productive district teacher evaluation systems. These elements bear a striking similarity to our keys to growth. First, the Stanford researchers hold that four enabling conditions provide the foundation of effective evaluation systems: mutual trust between teachers and administrators; open channels of communication that indeed are open; general commitment to the individual and institutional learning; and high level of awareness of the evaluation activities and associated learning efforts. Second, they outline several pivotal considerations in designing evaluation systems:

- Teachers and administrators should be jointly trained in the principles and procedures of the evaluation process so as to understand each other's roles;
- A system of checks and balances is needed to ensure validity and reliability, promote fairness, and give teachers a sense of safety in risk taking;
- Supervisors should be held accountable for conducting and reporting sound, growth-producing evaluations;
- The evaluation should be characterized by effective feedback—feedback that is timely, specific, credible, and perceived as nonpunitive;
- Evaluations are most appropriately driven by the teacher's goals and basic instructional strategies rather than by a fixed evaluation form or instrument;
- Rather than isolated from one another, as they are traditionally, districtwide evaluation and staff development re-

sources and mechanisms are integrated to promote development in areas uncovered by evaluation.

And finally, McLaughlin and Pfeifer point out how important it
is to be aware of the complexity of the process of teacher improvement:

> Individual improvement has at least two components: one, *re-
> flection* about teaching and areas of strength and weakness; and
> two, *motivation* to change, or to act on the results of reflection.
> But if individual improvement is to result in institutional im-
> provement, individual goals and development efforts must have
> a third characteristic: a high level of *integration* with district
> goals and priorities. District plans, then, must acknowledge
> these three aspects of improvement if improvement is to occur at
> the institutional level. (pp. 89–90 emphasis in original)

Because McLaughlin and Pfeifer approach the evaluation process from the direction of organizational change, their guidelines deal most directly with the promotion of an effective evaluation context. However, they also comment specifically on the
teacher–principal relationship, attributes of effective feedback,
and evaluation procedures, as we do. Thus, their guidelines
parallel our five keys.

After reflecting on approximately 300 teacher evaluation systems with which he had worked as a consultant, McGreal
(1986) identified nine commonalities that have emerged to represent a set of best practices:

1. *Attitudes.* Sound systems are built around the positive attitudes and procedures needed to promote instructional improvement rather than the negative attitudes and procedures associated with evaluation for accountability and
   teacher dismissal.
2. *Complementary procedures, processes, and instrumentation.* Evaluation procedures are flexible, allowing supervisors and teachers to tailor data collection to the individual
   needs of teachers.
3. *Separation of teacher evaluation from teaching evaluation.* Evaluation systems are most effective when they deal
   with specific dimensions of classroom instruction and
   teaching behaviors that can be improved; they are least

effective when they focus on performance criteria that are more administrative or personal in nature.

4. *Goal setting.* Effective, growth-producing evaluation systems replace the standardized criteria of accountability evaluation with individualized professional development goals, identified by teachers and supervisors.

5. *Narrowed focus on teaching.* Sound evaluation systems are centered on an agreed upon and clearly articulated definition of teaching that gives the teacher and the supervisor a common frame of reference.

6. *Use of a modified clinical supervision format.* Helpful evaluation relies on preobservation planning, observation of specified behaviors, and a feedback conference.

7. *Use of alternative data sources.* Over and above classroom observations by the supervisor, evaluations can be based upon self-evaluation, peer evaluation, parent evaluation, student evaluation, student performance, and examination of classroom artifacts.

8. *Different requirements for tenured and nontenured teachers.* The purposes for evaluation differ in fundamental ways, so should the evaluation procedures.

9. *A complete training program.* All participating teachers and supervisors must possess the skills and understanding needed to carry out an evaluation that will serve the growth purpose, which requires training.

By suggesting that these commonalities represent a point of departure for reviewing local evaluation practices, McGreal reinforces the point that we do not need further refinements of traditional accountability-driven evaluation systems. He asserts, as we do, that flexible, individualized, teacher-centered evaluation is essential for professional development to occur.

Rather than professional development, the focus for Bridges (1986) is how to deal with the incompetent teacher. The research is based on case studies, interviews, and surveys of instances in which districts sought to dismiss teachers. Specific and detailed guidelines are provided for satisfying technical and legal problems associated with dismissal of teachers who fail to meet minimum performance standards. In short, he deals specifically with the accountability side of the teacher evaluation equation. But even in this context, practical suggestions are advanced for conducting "salvage attempts." These suggestions correspond, to a certain extent, to the keys to growth outlined in previous chapters. According to Bridges, the probability of saving an incompetent teacher increases when the evaluation and supervision cycle is characterized by clear and honest criticism, clear behavioral specifications of changes needed in the teacher's performance, the development of an individualized remediation plan, and the provision of specific assistance to the failing teacher. Assistance might include opportunities to visit classes of outstanding teachers, access to special consultants, opportunities to attend workshops and special classes, and/or help in dealing with specific personal problems. Bridges' point is that remediation focuses on the individual and specific needs of the incompetent teacher. Our point is that the same focus can benefit competent teachers in their pursuit of excellence.

Research conducted by Dornbusch, Deal, Plumley, and Roper (1976) contributed important insights regarding effective strategies for making evaluation both relevant and helpful for teachers. One result of this research was the Stanford Collegial Evaluation Program, which, once completed, was shelved as an idea whose time had not yet come. Recently, that work has been revived by Roper and Hoffman (1986). These researchers argue for a multidimensional approach to teacher evaluation. In such a system, teachers and students become valued sources of evaluative feedback, and teacher self-assessment serves as a central component of the professional development process. The original field test of this system produced very positive results. Teachers chose partners, developed performance criteria relevant to their classroom, gathered observational data, tapped student opinion, provided feedback in conferences, and established ongoing working relationships. These researchers found, as we did, that teachers can grow as a result of this kind of meaningful evaluation.

In their recent work, Natriello and Wilson (1986) followed the line of inquiry pursued by Dornbusch and Scott (1975) and Wise et al. (1984) to reveal some of the influences of the context on the impact of teacher evaluation. Natriello and Wilson explored the relationship between teachers' perceptions of the ingredients in their evaluation and the utility of that evaluation under conditions of varying teacher influence in school decision making. Their conclusions about the role of teachers in the decision-making processes are clear and consistent with our conclusions:

> The evaluation process variables accounted for more variation in the soundness or utility of evaluations when schools were characterized by more teacher influence than when they were characterized by less teacher influence. This finding, along with the finding that more teacher influence over the curriculum and resources in a school leads to evaluations of greater utility, suggests that the degree of teacher influence in a school affects the operation of systems for the evaluation of teaching both by affecting the outcome of evaluation processes on the soundness and utility of evaluations and through more direct effects on the soundness and utility of evaluations. (p. 15)

In yet another study of teacher evaluation procedures, Stark and Lowther (1984) report the results of a survey of the opinions and preferences of nearly a thousand teachers. The opinions expressed provide a startlingly clear picture of the kinds of evaluative feedback teachers find appropriate:

> Self-Assessment clearly was viewed by the teacher subjects as the most appropriate method of evaluation; about 89 percent of the teachers either agreed or strongly agreed that teachers should assess their own work. Surprisingly, however, administrator judgments were also viewed by teachers as appropriate. About 85 percent of the teachers agreed or strongly agreed that classroom observations by administrators should be used, and 77 percent were accepting of administrator judgments regarding personal growth. Close behind in order of acceptance were Teacher Peer Assessment and assessment of Objectives Accomplished; 73–75 percent of the teachers accepted these modes of evaluation.
> Teachers viewed both the assessment of Test Results and Student/Parent Judgments in teacher evaluation negatively. From 52 percent to 79 percent of the teachers felt that the use of these modes of evaluation was not appropriate. Within the sets of items comprising these measures, locally constructed tests were viewed somewhat more favorably than standardized tests and student evaluations were viewed more favorably than parent evaluations. (p. 97)

In planning teacher evaluations, teacher preferences represent only one of many criteria that should be used in determining the kinds of data to gather. When the purpose for evaluation is accountability and personnel management, teacher preferences may not be one of the most important criteria. But when the purpose of evaluation is teacher growth, one of the keys to success is that teachers find the evaluative data to be believable and useful. Thus, in this case, teacher preferences for data are a key consideration. The Stark and Lowther data suggest, as do ours, that administrator judgments are important but not sufficient. Peer review and systematic self-assessment focused on negotiated professional development objectives also are important evaluation ingredients.

Summary of Parallel Research

Accumulating evidence from many sources suggests that teacher evaluation can be a very useful teacher improvement tool. However, if it is to reach its potential, specific evaluation conditions must be satisfied. Those conditions have been outlined by several researchers based on their independent investigations of local teacher evaluation procedures. While each research team chooses its own labels for the keys to success, the ingredients remain quite constant. Those ingredients include teachers and supervisors who regard each other as professionals working together in an environment of trust to gather systematic data on performance, share relevant feedback, and undertake individually relevant professional development programs.

Productive Research Methodology

Given the commonality of results from these independent lines of inquiry, it becomes quite clear that the next step in teacher evaluation research is to revise teacher evaluation systems to maximize their growth-producing potential and evaluate the impact. The kind of research methodology most likely to be productive in exploring and understanding issues related to implementation of effective growth-oriented evaluation systems is district case-study methodology. Only through in-depth observation, interview, and interpretation of experience can we (a) understand the conditions that bring a district to the point of developing a growth system, (b) learn what specific types of training will give educators the skills and confidence needed to bring such a system into existence, (c) observe and describe the changes in teaching and learning precipitated by a growth-oriented evaluation, and (d) explore the implications of such a system in the ongoing political and social context of schools. In-depth case studies have proven to be an immensely powerful tool in the research reported in this volume, and they will continue to be the methodology of choice in implementation studies of the future.

The Role of the TEP

Within the context of studying districts in the process of developing new evaluation systems, the Teacher Evaluation Profile (TEP) instrument may be a valuable tool. It is capable of providing valid, reliable, and sensitive information about key aspects of the teacher evaluation process. The results can be gathered and analyzed in a cost effective manner and can be communicated clearly to decision makers.

The validity of the instrument was established during its development. The items and scales were written to reflect keys to growth-producing evaluation, as described by teachers who benefited from such evaluations. The utility of the information provided by the TEP has been established in subsequent field applications of the instrument in districts considering change. The reliability of the resulting data has been explored from the perspective of internal consistency and the results have been very positive, as reported in Chapter 5. Initial applications also suggest that the TEP is a powerful enough microscope to detect meaningful differences in teacher evaluation environments across districts. Results can be reported at the level of individual items or scale scores that have a clear meaning and relevance to users. Finally, as a paper and pencil questionnaire with rating-scale responses, the instrument can be distributed, completed, and analyzed in an economical manner. The TEP is a technically sound research tool.

The TEP would be useful in at least three contexts. The first is in diagnosing particular problems associated with teacher evaluation in local school districts. Given a profile summarizing teachers' responses to each of the items on the TEP, districts can identify those items in which teacher ratings appear particularly inappropriate. These data, considered along with information on which items are most predictive of a growth-producing impact of evaluation in any particular district, could lead to specific decisions regarding where to begin to revise evaluation procedures in that district.

A second application of the TEP is in evaluating the impact of changes in teacher evaluation systems. When administered on a pre–post-evaluation basis or in time series, TEP can yield scale scores that represent an excellent means of tracking the impact of system changes on teachers' perceptions of their evaluations.

Yet another use of the TEP is in comparisons of different evaluation environments, such as in comparing schools, districts, or evaluation systems designed to serve different purposes. Whether in applied local teacher evaluation research or the broader arena of more theoretical research on the principles of sound teacher evaluation, the TEP represents an excellent dependent measure.

As users apply the TEP in research and evaluation contexts, however, they are encouraged to explore its refinement. Several key issues deserve further attention. For instance, while we were able to quite accurately predict the overall quality and impact ratings using questionnaire items and the five scales (see Chapter 5), the multiple correlations were far from perfect. Thus, there may well be other key factors yet to be discovered. Researchers investigating additional examples of productive evaluations could identify additional factors that contribute to success.

More attention also needs to be devoted to defining indicators of the impact of evaluation. We used a teacher self-report index of impact. Might supervisors or colleagues provide additional insights as to the impact of evaluation on a particular teacher? Why did teachers in our studies so consistently rate the quality of their evaluations higher than the impact and what are the implications of differences? Is there a role for student achievement in an index of impact? These issues related to the definition of impact deserve further investigation.

A third measurement issue in need of further research is: How should researchers summarize and present the results of the TEP in a manner that would help district decision makers understand and use questionnaire results? For instance, how can standards or norms be established, and would they be helpful? How can local decision makers relate results specifically to the program-development decisions they face? As local implementation case studies are conducted, these issues need to be addressed.

The Research Agenda

In summary, two themes appear to characterize the research agenda for growth-oriented teacher evaluation. First, there is a need for case studies of the implementation of growth-oriented evaluation systems. Under what conditions are teachers and districts willing to change? What training is needed? Do anticipated changes occur? What is the impact of the changes on the evaluation process, on teachers and on students?

The second theme is replication. More case studies of successful evaluations are needed—studies of districts conducting effective evaluation systems and studies of teachers whose professional development has been enhanced through effective evaluation. Our research results and the TEP are based on a limited number of cases. The external validity of those case-study results has not yet been established. The TEP may profit from further technical analysis. The confidence we have in the evaluation process and its impact on teacher improvement will grow as we accumulate corroborating evidence. As that evidence is accumulating, however, there are actions we can take to improve current evaluation policy and practice. We address those in the seventh and final chapter.

SEVEN

Implications for Policy and Practice

Educational research is most satisfying when it can be used to improve the school experiences of students and teachers. The research presented in previous chapters has the potential to enhance the meaningfulness of teaching and to benefit student learning. The final chapter examines some of the practical implications of this teacher evaluation research.

The case studies of positive teacher evaluation experiences discussed in Chapters 3 and 4 indicate that teachers are interested in and capable of professional improvement. Teachers acknowledge the value of performance evaluation and supervision, if it is done well. Given the right conditions and encouragement, they can acquire new skills, attitudes, and understanding. What questions, then, must policy makers address in order to promote teacher evaluation practices that truly are growth oriented?

Evaluation Systems

The first question for policy makers is *Can evaluation systems promote teacher growth?* The question is important because evaluation systems are required by law in many states, in order to ensure professional accountability. Many educators voice skepticism, however, over the likelihood that these systems also can contribute to professional development, particularly for veteran teachers. Their reasons include concern that supervisors cannot serve simultaneously as helpers and evaluators and fear that teachers interested in improvement may risk personnel action by disclosing weaknesses.

Our research suggests that evaluation systems can promote teacher growth, but only under certain conditions. These conditions are that (a) the accountability system remains somewhat independent of the growth system, and (b) the systems for evaluating new and probationary teachers remain distinct from the system for monitoring the performance of competent, experienced teachers.

It may help policy makers to think in terms of three parallel evaluation systems: one for new and untenured teachers; one for competent experienced teachers; and one for experienced teachers with deficiencies. Table 16 presents salient dimensions of these three systems.

The Induction System is intended to evaluate the extent to which new teachers have mastered basic performance standards. Such standards need to cover such areas as lesson design, delivery of instruction, assessment of student progress, and classroom management. Presumably, no teacher would be tenured or given a continuing contract who failed to demonstrate competence in these key areas. To monitor and evaluate performance in the Induction System, supervisors would need to observe teachers on a regular basis, offer plenty of feedback, and provide encouragement in areas of strength and assistance in areas of weakness.

The Remediation System serves another purpose, but one linked more to accountability than growth. This system is designed to address the needs of experienced teachers who, for whatever reason, have slipped below the minimum level of acceptable performance in a given performance standard. With dismissal a possible consequence of failure to correct a deficiency, the Remediation System must safeguard the due-process rights of teachers. Toward this end, provisions should exist for official notification of the need for remediation (letter of reprimand) and specification of a plan to correct deficiencies (plan of assistance). It typically is a school district's responsibility to provide resources to help deficient teachers raise performance to acceptable levels.

The evaluation needs of many, if not most, teachers are not served by either the Induction System or the Remediation System. These experienced individuals already have mastered the

Table 16

Parallel Evaluation Systems

	Induction System	Remediation System	Professional Development System
Target Group	New teachers	Experienced teachers in need of remediation	Competent experienced teachers
Focus	Mastering performance standards	Correcting deficiency in performance standard	Pursuit of excellence in selected areas of instruction, etc.
			Meet the challenge of particular students
Purpose	Need to achieve tenure or continuing contract status	Avoid dismissal	Need to continue growing as a professional
Procedures and Mechanisms	Clinical supervision	Letter of reprimand	Goal setting
	Annual evaluation of performance standards	Informal assistance	Clinical supervision
	Induction classes	Formal plan of assistance	Reliance on many sources of performance data (supervisor, peers, student; and self)
	Mentors	Remediation team	
	Recognize similarities in performance expectations for all teachers	Clinical supervision	Recheck performance standards periodically (every three or four years)
			Recognize differences in performance expectations for different grade levels, subject areas

basic performance standards and they continue to teach competently. For them, a system is required that will encourage continued professional development. Such a system must be flexible enough to permit teachers to grow in different ways. While the Induction System is designed to raise the performance of all new teachers to at least a minimum level of adequacy, the Professional Development System should provide opportunities for different teachers to become virtuoso performers in different aspects of teaching. While one teacher might study dramatics in order to become a spellbinding lecturer, another might develop exceptional skill in diagnosing student learning difficulties. There is no reason why all teachers should continue to develop in identical ways, once basic performance standards have been mastered. The mechanism best suited to the Professional Development System is individual goal setting. Teachers can negotiate improvement plans that best fit their individual needs as professionals.

It is possible, of course, for competent veterans to decline in their skills. For this reason, Professional Development Systems must make provision for periodic checks to determine whether basic performance standards still are being met. There is little reason to undertake these check-ups annually or even biennially, however. To do so is to squander the precious time of supervisors and communicate distrust to teachers. The Remediation System always is available for emergencies, if a teacher's performance should decline precipitously between check ups.

Policies Supporting Growth

Nearly all available research on teacher evaluation suggests that evaluations are most productive when conducted in a district environment publicly committed to teacher growth. When that commitment is apparent from the very top of the organizational chart, all involved can take the risk of making their professional development needs known. The best way to make that commitment to teacher growth public and apparent to all is through clear statements of policy. Therefore, a key question for policy makers is *What policies are needed to support growth-oriented teacher evaluation?*

The most important policy decision involves the differentiation of the evaluation processes for new teachers, competent experienced teachers, and experienced teachers with deficiencies. These three parallel systems were outlined in the preceding section. Additional policy decisions also are needed to determine who will be involved in the evaluation process and the frequency of evaluations.

Even the most carefully designed evaluation system may fail to achieve its purpose when those subject to evaluation are denied a role in developing the system. Research by Natriello and Wilson (1986) confirms that teacher involvement in developing evaluation systems increases the likelihood that these systems will be perceived positively. Furthermore, for teaching to be regarded as a true profession, teachers must play an active role in determining the criteria and procedures by which they will be evaluated (Myers, 1973, pp. 19–29). In fact, one potentially valuable source of professional growth would seem to be involvement in the development and periodic refinement of basic performance standards for teaching. Such an undertaking would require participants to review the latest research on teaching and deliberate the essential skills and knowledge needed to teach.

In light of the preceding points, school district policy should require and promote teacher participation in the development of teacher evaluation systems. In addition, since no system can be expected to remain effective forever, policy should provide for teacher participation in the periodic assessment and modification of these evaluation systems.

The frequency of teacher evaluation is an additional policy issue, the resolution of which can exert a major impact on the growth-producing potential of the evaluation system. If competent veterans must be evaluated in light of the basic performance standards on a yearly basis, the time available for growth-oriented evaluation and goal setting may be reduced severely. As long as provisions exist for placing experienced teachers on remedial programs in case of obvious deficiencies, there is little need for annual evaluations based on the performance standards of the Induction System. Where competent veterans are concerned, evaluation for accountability purposes probably need occur no more frequently than every four years. During the years when these teachers are not being evaluated for minimum competence, they are free to participate in professional development activities. To further encourage growth during these times, a policy may be needed to minimize or prevent formal documentation. Growth entails risk, and teachers may be more willing to take risks if they know that evaluation will be private and undocumented.

If evaluation during periods of professional development is kept separate from evaluation designed to ensure accountability, evaluation that is driven by basic performance standards, then there is no reason why a variety of people cannot be involved in the process of collecting and sharing evaluation data. Our research indicated that peers, department heads, central office supervisors, outside consultants, and students could make important contributions to professional development. If district policy encouraged the involvement of these individuals, principals would be free to spend more time with new teachers and experienced teachers deficient in one or more performance standards. If nonadministrators are to play a role in evaluation, it is crucial, of course, that they receive adequate training.

Training

Our research demonstrates that the success of teacher evaluation often is a function of the skill, knowledge, and attitudes of both teachers and supervisors. *What specific training and preparation are required in order to promote growth-oriented evaluation?*

The most valuable knowledge for supervisors and teachers is a vision of good instruction. A vision can be based on research or derived from a coherent set of values and aspirations. With it, supervisors and teachers are more likely to understand what they are striving to accomplish. Without a common vision to guide them, the interactions of supervisors and teachers may degenerate into the exchange of anecdotes and vague impressions.

Vision, though, is of little value if it cannot be communicated effectively. Effective communication depends on more than a clear set of descriptive terms and good speaking ability. Teachers told us that they often are unable or unwilling to hear what supervisors have to say because trust and credibility are lacking. Some supervisors overlook the fact that effective communication requires listening as well as talking. Since there is no reason to assume that supervisors and teachers automatically possess the skills necessary to work with each other productively, training in interpersonal relations and communications is an essential component of any plan for growth-oriented teacher evaluation.

Besides vision and communication skills, supervisors and teachers need technical training in the collection and analysis of descriptive data on teaching. Data collection may entail the design and use of instruments for coding, counting, rating, checking, and mapping behaviors. Training in the use of audiovisual equipment and the recording of verbatim notes also may be helpful. The analysis of data may require individuals to identify behavior patterns, create ratios for comparisons across classes and time periods, and collect supplementary information on student achievement.

It is important to note that we have stressed that *both* supervisors and teachers should receive evaluation training. We believe it is insufficient to do as many states and districts have done and require training only for supervisors. Such a course of action perpetuates the idea that evaluation is something done *to* teachers. If teacher evaluation is to contribute to growth, teachers as well as supervisors must be well versed in the process. Both must understand the components of good teaching, master the skills of interpersonal communication, and know how to make sense of data collected on teaching. Such knowledge increases the likelihood that teachers eventually will become the agents of their own professional development, rather than remaining dependent on others.

Diverse Data Sources

Training supervisors and teachers in the techniques of data collection should stress the availability of various sources of valuable information on teaching. *What types of data can contribute to teacher growth?*

The most frequently used source of data probably is classroom observation. Observers may attempt to focus on a narrow range of behavior, such as teacher questions or off-task student conduct, or they may try to comprehend everything occurring during a given time. Observations may be descriptive or impressionistic. The period of observation may last for a few minutes, as in the case of an informal drop-in, or an entire lesson or period. In certain cases, observers may decide to visit the same class two or three days in a row. A variety of observation techniques and instruments are available to facilitate the data-collection process.

While extremely valuable, observational data represent just

one of many potential sources of information. Not all meaning-ful phenomena can be easily observed. For example, to deter-mine how well students are learning what they are expected to learn, student achievement data are needed. Examples of stu-dent performance on seatwork, projects, homework, quizzes and tests are potentially helpful. Teachers and/or observers on occasion may want to ask students direct questions regarding material covered in class. To assess the transfer of learning, data also may be needed on student performance in subsequent classes or learning situations.

To understand the key role student achievement data can play in teacher evaluation, we need to remain keenly aware of what kinds of data are used by whom and for what purpose. To begin, measurement experts and professional educators alike agree that it is unsound practice to use norm-referenced stan-dardized achievement test scores in conducting evaluations of teachers (Haertel, 1986). There are two sound reasons for this. First, these tests are too imprecise (i.e., brief and superficial) to serve as valid performance criteria. They cannot test enough of what is taught to be a fair basis for evaluating a teacher's per-formance. Second, too many factors on these tests are beyond the control of the teacher (e.g. student aptitude, home learning environment, and the impact of prior teachers) influence stu-dent scores to attribute the scores to the work of one teacher.

Here we arrive at a paradox. We know that norm-referenced standardized student achievement test scores provide an inad-equate basis upon which to evaluate teachers, yet we also know that one key index of the quality of teaching, in fact, is student learning. So, do we ignore student achievement in evaluating teachers? Definitely not. However, we approach the data and their use from a different direction. If we are careful to give teachers the know-how and the tools to measure and keep track of student growth on a day-to-day and week-to-week basis, and if we place teachers in charge of gathering, analyzing, and pre-senting evidence of the growth of students using teacher-devel-oped and text-embedded classroom assessments, then teachers will be in a better position to identify teaching approaches that promote student achievement. On the basis of these results, teachers and their supervisors can detect areas of instruction in which the teachers need further professional development.

In short, student achievement data can play a key role in teacher evaluation if the data are (a) sensitive to day-to-day instructional priorities, (b) used by the teacher and the supervisor working together, and (c) used to promote teacher improvement. To reach this goal, both the supervisor and the teacher may have to think about how to improve their level of confidence and expertise in the measurement of student achievement.

Students can provide useful data on other aspects of instruction besides their own achievement. For example, no one is in a better position to comment on the clarity of teacher directions than the students for whom the directions are intended. Students are the only observers who are in class on a regular basis. As a result, they are in a unique position to comment on important dimensions of their learning environment. As long as they are not asked to comment on aspects of teaching for which they lack expertise, students constitute a rich source of data for professional development.

Artifacts are yet another source of data. They may include examples of teacher work, such as course syllabi, lesson plans, tests, grade books, classroom rules and procedures, notes to students, and referral slips. Student work, including course notes, projects, and homework, also can provide insights regarding teaching effectiveness.

Another source of data is the teacher. The fields of psychology, psychotherapy, and philosophy are based, in part, on the belief that individuals possess important knowledge about themselves. This knowledge may be essential for self-understanding and growth. To be revealed, such knowledge often requires the involvement of a good listener or special training in systematic reflection.

The point of this section is to encourage reliance on many types of data in evaluating teaching. Our research suggests that professional development can result from exposure to various types of information. It is unlikely that any one source of data will be equally beneficial or persuasive for all teachers, or even for any particular teacher over the course of a career.

A Culture Conducive to Growth

A final set of recommendations from our research addresses the question of organizational context. *What school culture is most capable of supporting and sustaining teacher growth?*

Our research suggests that teacher evaluation is unlikely to be a high priority in school districts that have failed to develop an effective accountability system for dealing with incompetent or marginally competent teachers. The existence of a mature accountability-based evaluation process assures teachers that their property and due process rights will be honored and protects the public from unqualified instructors. With key rights and obligations ensured, educators are free to dedicate time and resources to teacher evaluation that is improvement oriented.

Another key element of school culture that promotes teacher growth is teacher involvement in decision making. Teachers who play central roles in development of evaluation procedures are more likely to trust and benefit from those procedures. Teachers can and should participate in decisions regarding performance standards, evaluation procedures, and resources needed for improvement. It is easier to foster a climate of trust when school administrators provide teachers access to these decisions.

A third important characteristic of improvement-oriented school cultures is the availability of resources to support professional development. It is of little value for teachers and supervisors to identify areas in need of improvement if local boards are unwilling to provide released time, tuition reimbursement, visitation days, learning materials, videotape equipment, peer coaches, and other necessary resources. If high-quality teaching is truly valued by a school system, the district should share the expense associated with professional development.

Conclusion

Our goal throughout the research summarized in this book has been to make teacher evaluation as meaningful as possible for teachers and supervisors. No one benefits when teacher–supervisor conferences, data collection, goal setting, professional development workshops, and written evaluations degenerate into meaningless rituals. We have suggested that most teachers will regard evaluation and related processes as meaningful when they perceive that personal and professional growth results from them. For teacher evaluation to promote growth, we further have argued that changes must take place in (a) the policies governing evaluation, (b) the training of supervisors and teachers, (c) the types of data collected on teacher performance, and (d) the cultural contexts in which evaluations are conducted. While these recommendations constitute an ambitious agenda, we believe that the current interest in educational reform provides the impetus necessary to effect substantive changes.

Appendix A

Teacher Evaluation Profile (TEP) Questionnaire:*

This form has been designed to allow you to describe your experience with teacher evaluation in some detail. Your responses will be combined with those of other teachers to yield a clearer picture of the key ingredients in an effective teacher evaluation experience. The goal of this research is to determine if and how the evaluation process can be revised to help it serve relevant and useful purposes. If we are to reach this goal, it will be important for you to provide frank and honest responses. This is why your answers will remain anonymous.

As you will see, this is not a superficial questionnaire. It is designed to be comprehensive in scope and will take more than a few minutes to complete. For this reason, it is crucial that you read and follow directions very carefully. Please set aside twenty uninterrupted minutes to provide thoughtful responses.

The Definition of Teacher Evaluation

Guidelines for teacher evaluation in the state of Oregon specify that every probationary teacher must be evaluated annually and every tenured teacher must be evaluated biennially. The process leading to the end-of-the-year evaluation is expected to consist of goal setting, classroom observation, and conferences between teacher and supervisor before and after the observation. When reference is made in this questionnaire to *teacher evaluation*, it should be understood to encompass all these elements.

---

*This is the research version of the TEP. Subsequent revisions have resulted in the development of a more effective and efficient version of the questionnaire. Scoring and reporting services have also been developed. For details, contact the Northwest Regional Educational Laboratory, 101 SW Main St., Suite 500, Portland, OR 97204.

Specific Instructions

Given this definition of teacher evaluation, please reflect on the last time you were evaluated—your *most recent* experience with a teacher evaluation system. Regard the entire evaluation process, including planning for evaluation, classroom observations, and feedback. As you think about this experience, how woul you rate the *overall quality* of the evaluation? Use a scale from 0 to 9, with 0 representing poor quality and 9 high quality.

Now please enter your response on the computer response form that you have been given by following these instructions:

- Find the side of the form that says "Part 1" under the example in the upper right corner.
- Then find the ID number box in the upper left corner.
- Using a number 2 pencil, please code your Rating of Overall Quality on the *top line* of the I.D. Number box. Be sure to *blacken* the entire space associated with each response as shown below.

⊏0⊐ ⊏1⊐ ⊏2⊐ ⊏3⊐ ⊏4⊐ ⊏5⊐ ⊏6⊐ ⊏7⊐ ⊏8⊐ ⊏9⊐	↗
⊏0⊐ ⊏1⊐ ⊏2⊐ ⊏3⊐ ⊏4⊐ ⊏5⊐ ⊏6⊐ ⊏7⊐ ⊏8⊐ ⊏9⊐	WRITE
⊏0⊐ ⊏1⊐ ⊏2⊐ ⊏3⊐ ⊏4⊐ ⊏5⊐ ⊏6⊐ ⊏7⊐ ⊏8⊐ ⊏9⊐	I.D.
⊏0⊐ ⊏1⊐ ⊏2⊐ ⊏3⊐ ⊏4⊐ ⊏5⊐ ⊏6⊐ ⊏7⊐ ⊏8⊐ ⊏9⊐	NUMBER
⊏0⊐ ⊏1⊐ ⊏2⊐ ⊏3⊐ ⊏4⊐ ⊏5⊐ ⊏6⊐ ⊏7⊐ ⊏8⊐ ⊏9⊐	HERE

Next, please rate the *impact* of that teacher evaluation on three specific aspects of your professional practice. Use the next three lines in the I.D. Number box to code your rating for each, from 0 meaning no impact to 9 meaning strong impact:

- On the second line from the top, code the *impact on your attitudes* about teaching: A strong impact rating of (9) would reflect a profound change in how you feel about the content you teach, your students, and/or yourself as a teacher.
- On the third line, code the *impact on your teaching behaviors and strategies:* A strong impact (9) would reflect major changes in your instructional behavior, classroom managements strategies, evaluation practices, and/or other observable dimensions of your teaching.
- On the fourth line from the top, code the *impact on your understanding of the teaching/learning process:* A strong impact (9) would reflect a change in your ability to account

for your effectiveness (or lack thereof), explain the reasons for your instructional decisions, and/or, better understanding of student needs or behavior.

At this point, you should have coded your ratings of the evaluation experience (overall and three impacts) on the top four lines of the ID number box. Leave the remaining lines in the ID box blank.

Now, please use the scales provided on the following pages to describe yourself and the nature of your *most recent* teacher evaluation. Do this by

● Considering the attribute to be described,
● Studying the scale to be used to describe it,
● Selecting the letter that represents the point you select on each scale, and
● Coding that letter on the response form.

Be sure the number of the attribute you are describing corresponds to the number on the response sheet where you enter your response.

A. *Describe These Attributes of You as a Teacher*

1. Rate your overall competence as a teacher — I'm minimally competent A B C D E I'm an outstanding teacher

2. Rate the strength of your professional expectations of yourself — I demand little A B C D E I demand a great deal

Describe your interpersonal manner:

3. Orientation to risk taking — I avoid risks A B C D E I take risks

4. Orientation to others — I'm reserved, private A B C D E I'm open, public

5. Attribution of reasons for your success/failure — I hold others responsible A B C D E I hold myself responsible

6. Orientation to change — I'm relatively slow to change A B C D E I'm relatively flexible

7. Orientation to experimentation in classroom — I don't experiment A B C D E I experiment frequently

8. Openness to criticism — I'm relatively closed A B C D E I'm relatively open

9. Knowledge of technical aspects of teaching — I know a little A B C D E I know a great deal

10. Knowledge of subject matter   I know a little A B C D E I know a great deal

Describe your teaching experience:

11. At current grade

A:	0 to 1 year
B:	2 to 3 years
C:	4 to 5 years
D:	6 to 10 years
E:	11 or more years

12. With current content
    (if secondary teacher)

A:	0 to 1 year
B:	2 to 3 years
C:	4 to 5 years
D:	6 to 10 years
E:	11 or more years

13. Experience with teacher evaluation
    prior to most recent experience   Waste of time A B C D E Helpful

B. Describe Your Perceptions of Person Who Evaluated Your Performance (Most Recently)

14. Credibility as a source of feedback   Not credible A B C D E Very credible

15. Working relationship with you   Adversary A B C D E Helper

16. Level of trust   Not trustworthy A B C D E Trustworthy

17. Interpersonal manner   Threatening A B C D E Not threatening

18. Temperament   Impatient A B C D E Patient

19. Flexibility   Rigid A B C D E Flexible

20. Knowledge of technical aspects of
    teaching   Not knowledgeable A B C D E Knowledgeable

21. Capacity to demonstrate or model
    needed improvements   Low A B C D E High

22. Familiarity with your particular class-
    room   Unfamiliar A B C D E Very familiar

23. Experience in classrooms in general   Little A B C D E A great deal

24. Usefulness of suggestions for improve-
    ments   Useless A B C D E Useful

25. Persuasiveness of rationale for sug-
    gestions   Not persuasive A B C D E Very persuasive

C. Describe These Attributes of the Information Gathered on Your Performance During Your Most Recent Evaluation

How were the dimensions of your teaching (standards) to be evaluated/addressed?

26. Were standards communicated to you?　　　　Not at all A B C D E In great detail

27. Were standards clear to you?　　　　Vague A B C D E Clear

28. Were standards endorsed by you as appropriate for your classroom?　　　　Not endorsed A B C D E Endorsed

29. What was the form of the standards?
   A:　Goals to be attained
   B:　Personal and/or professional traits to possess
   C:　Both

30. Were the standards　　The same for all teachers? A B C D E　Unique to you?

To what extent were the following sources of performance information tapped as part of the evaluation?

31. Observation of your classroom performance　　Not considered A B C D E Used extensively

32. Examination of classroom or school records (lesson plans, etc.)　　Not considered A B C D E Used extensively

33. Examination of student achievement　　Not considered A B C D E Used extensively

To what extent were there observations in your classroom?
(Note: In these items. *formal* refers to observations that were preannounced and were preceded and followed by a conference with the evaluator: *informal* refers to unannounced drop-in visits)

34. Number of formal observations per year (most recent experience)
   A:　0
   B:　1
   C:　2
   D:　3
   E:　4 or more

35. Approximate frequency of informal observations (most recent experience)
   A:　None
   B:　Less than 1 per month
   C:　Once per month
   D:　Once per week
   E:　Daily

What was the average length of observation (most recent experience)?

36. Formal　　Brief (few minutes) A B C D E Extended (40 minutes or more)

			Extended	
		Brief	(40 minutes	
37. Informal		(few minutes) A B C D E	or more)	

38. Number of different people observing   A: Supervisor only
     and evaluating you during the year   B: Supervisor & 1 other person
                                         C: Supervisor & 2 other persons
                                         D: Supervisor & 3 or more
                                         E: Other

If others besides your supervisor evaluated _____
you, who were they (titles only)?   _____

D. Describe These Attributes of the Feedback You Received

39. Amount of information received
                                     None   A B C D E   Great deal

40. Frequency of formal feedback   Infrequent   A B C D E   Frequent

41. Frequency of informal feedback
                              Infrequent   A B C D E   Frequent

42. Depth of information provided
                               Shallow   A B C D E   In-depth

43. Quality of the ideas and suggestions
     contained in the feedback   Low   A B C D E   High

44. Specificity of information provided   General   A B C D E   Specific

45. Nature of information provided   Judgmental   A B C D E   Descriptive

46. Timing of the feedback   Delayed   A B C D E   Immediate

47. Feedback focused on district teaching
     standards   Ignored them   A B C D E   Reflected them

E. Describe These Attributes of the Evaluation Context

48. Amount of time spent on the evalua-
     tion process, including your time and
     that of all other participants   None   A B C D E   Great deal

What resources are available for professional development?

49. Time allotted during the teaching day
     for professional development   None   A B C D E   Great deal

50. Available training programs and
     models   None   A B C D E   Many

How were district values and policies expressed in evaluation?

51. Clarity of policy statements regarding
     purpose for evaluation   Vague   A B C D E   Clear

	Teacher		Teacher
52. Intended role of evaluation	accountability	A B C D E	growth
53. Recent history of labor relations in district	Turbulent	A B C D E	Tranquil
54. Impact of collective bargaining agreement on evaluation process	None	A B C D E	Great deal
55. Impact of state law on evaluation process	None	A B C D E	Great deal

F. Are there other dimensions of you as a teacher, the nature of the performance data collected, the nature of the feedback, the evaluation context, or other factors that you think are related to the success (or lack of success) of your past teacher evaluation experiences that should be included in the above list? If so, please specify.

_____

_____

_____

_____

_____

Appendix B

Item Means and Standard Deviations by District

Item Number	District 1 (n = 33)		District 2 (n = 71)		District 3 (n = 248)		District 4 (n = 64)		District 5 (n = 54)		Total (n = 470)	
	X̄	SD	X̄	SD	X̄	SD	X̄	SD	X̄	SD	X̄	SD
1	4.03	.47	4.41	.50	4.28	.59	4.30	.58	4.32	.58	4.29	.57
2	4.39	.66	4.61	.55	4.41	.69	4.53	.64	4.40	.63	4.45	.66
3	3.36	.86	3.82	.88	3.62	.89	3.72	.86	3.63	1.14	3.64	.92
4	3.49	1.00	3.62	1.06	3.54	1.08	3.55	1.04	3.78	1.06	3.58	1.06
5	4.36	.65	4.35	.83	4.42	.64	4.35	.77	4.51	.75	4.41	.70
6	3.85	.94	4.04	.87	4.06	.85	3.98	.88	4.32	.77	4.06	.86
7	3.85	.83	4.10	.72	3.89	.79	3.83	.75	4.07	1.01	3.93	.81
8	3.82	.88	3.68	.86	3.71	.86	3.83	.88	4.20	.81	3.78	.87
9	4.00	.76	4.17	.70	3.97	.80	4.11	.70	4.17	.69	4.04	.76
10	4.12	.70	4.45	.65	4.39	.64	4.32	.69	4.41	.57	4.37	.65
11	3.24	1.37	4.09	1.12	4.12	1.24	3.49	1.47	3.51	1.12	3.90	1.29
12	2.96	1.40	3.65	1.30	4.07	1.21	3.21	1.47	3.09	1.53	3.71	1.37
13	3.24	1.03	3.07	1.23	2.86	1.12	3.23	1.04	3.57	1.22	3.05	1.15
14	3.49	1.00	3.92	1.09	3.39	1.16	3.91	1.03	3.98	1.20	3.61	1.15
15	3.91	1.16	4.18	1.07	3.78	1.09	4.02	1.18	4.23	1.07	3.93	1.12
16	3.49	1.15	4.07	1.13	3.78	1.26	3.91	1.29	4.19	1.04	3.87	1.22
17	3.67	.96	4.14	1.05	3.92	1.10	4.13	1.07	4.23	1.15	4.00	1.09
18	3.46	1.12	3.83	1.10	3.99	1.00	4.18	1.03	4.26	.90	3.98	1.03
19	2.85	1.03	3.59	1.20	3.43	1.28	3.79	1.26	4.17	1.01	3.54	1.25
20	3.73	.76	3.89	.96	3.47	1.20	3.95	.96	4.06	1.12	3.69	1.12
21	3.13	1.18	3.41	1.02	2.92	1.23	3.34	1.09	3.64	1.33	3.15	1.22
22	3.24	1.09	3.54	1.12	2.85	1.19	3.40	.99	3.79	1.38	3.16	1.22
23	3.28	.92	3.76	.89	3.15	1.17	3.53	.90	4.13	1.09	3.42	1.12
24	3.18	1.07	3.70	1.01	3.18	1.13	3.52	1.06	3.83	1.32	3.38	1.15
25	3.13	.89	3.49	1.02	3.16	1.03	3.73	.99	3.66	1.19	3.35	1.06
26	4.00	.94	3.93	.93	3.32	1.10	3.44	.88	3.28	1.50	3.47	1.12
27	4.09	.95	4.09	1.07	3.42	1.18	3.65	.99	3.60	1.56	3.62	1.20
28	3.52	1.18	3.93	.94	3.59	1.09	3.78	1.08	3.35	1.58	3.63	1.15
29	2.15	1.00	2.47	.92	2.31	1.00	2.54	.86	2.56	.91	2.38	.96
30	3.03	1.45	2.71	1.46	3.08	1.38	2.63	1.49	2.64	1.43	2.91	1.43
31	4.46	.79	4.45	.86	3.34	1.21	4.25	.82	3.76	1.04	3.76	1.17
32	3.27	1.31	2.93	1.31	2.40	1.16	2.44	1.03	3.19	1.30	2.64	1.23
33	2.47	1.16	2.70	1.29	2.56	1.17	2.57	1.19	3.38	1.27	2.67	1.22
34	1.79	.96	1.86	1.11	1.27	.95	1.63	.87	1.09	1.10	1.42	1.02
35	2.52	.97	2.25	.72	2.25	.88	2.61	1.03	2.78	1.08	2.38	.93
36	4.09	1.03	4.25	.99	3.53	1.32	3.64	1.05	2.68	1.36	3.60	1.29
37	2.50	1.24	2.44	1.18	1.90	1.07	1.92	.95	1.61	.94	1.99	1.10
38	1.52	.83	1.49	.83	1.45	.73	1.36	.82	1.33	.59	1.43	.75
39	3.36	.78	3.58	1.05	3.00	1.06	3.52	.94	3.09	1.22	3.19	1.07
40	3.00	1.12	3.00	1.37	2.31	1.16	2.74	1.25	2.67	1.45	2.56	1.27
41	2.88	1.17	2.90	1.25	2.22	1.13	3.10	1.39	2.68	1.38	2.54	1.26

Appendix B (Cont.)

Item Means and Standard Deviations by District

Item Number	District 1 (n = 33)		District 2 (n = 71)		District 3 (n = 248)		District 4 (n = 64)		District 5 (n = 54)		Total (n = 470)	
	$\bar{X}$	SD	$\bar{X}$	SD	$\bar{X}$	SD	$\bar{X}$	SD	$\bar{X}$	SD	$\bar{X}$	SD
42	2.94	1.12	3.27	1.23	2.76	1.11	3.28	1.05	3.02	1.22	2.95	1.15
43	2.91	1.07	3.34	1.21	3.01	1.19	3.49	1.08	3.21	1.35	3.14	1.20
44	3.52	1.12	3.45	1.19	2.99	1.24	3.53	1.04	3.42	1.35	3.22	1.23
45	3.64	1.19	3.76	1.08	3.35	1.12	3.64	1.13	3.47	1.34	3.48	1.16
46	3.03	1.29	4.09	1.03	3.63	1.16	3.54	1.24	3.66	1.34	3.65	1.20
47	3.85	.97	4.11	1.03	3.48	1.12	3.62	1.02	3.56	1.15	3.63	1.11
48	3.33	.96	3.37	.95	3.17	.91	3.06	.88	2.85	1.12	3.16	.95
49	1.79	.78	1.87	1.10	2.10	.98	1.98	1.09	2.66	1.29	2.09	1.06
50	2.15	.94	2.50	1.11	2.54	1.07	2.33	1.02	2.80	1.28	2.51	1.09
51	3.52	1.12	3.61	1.33	3.38	1.09	3.30	1.04	3.15	1.54	3.38	1.18
52	1.94	1.03	3.22	1.24	3.02	1.26	3.39	1.18	3.43	1.49	3.07	1.30
53	1.38	.55	3.54	1.04	2.68	1.08	2.73	.94	2.62	1.30	2.72	1.16
54	2.69	1.20	2.69	1.17	2.97	1.06	2.24	1.02	2.41	1.34	2.75	1.15
55	3.23	.67	3.35	1.13	3.41	1.06	3.22	1.25	2.23	1.32	3.22	1.16
Overall	6.00	1.76	6.51	2.14	5.68	2.32	6.45	1.68	6.06	2.76	5.97	2.26
Attitude	3.57	2.25	4.70	2.54	4.35	2.40	4.74	2.53	6.08	3.13	4.58	2.57
Behavior	3.57	2.08	4.39	2.57	4.27	2.32	5.09	2.48	5.70	3.01	4.49	2.49
Understand	3.77	2.40	4.68	2.40	4.21	2.55	4.93	2.15	5.40	3.09	4.47	2.56

Appendix C

Largest Correlations Between Items and Criteria by District

	Overall Quality					Attitude					Behavior					Understanding				
	Dist. 1	Dist. 2	Dist. 3	Dist. 4	Dist. 5	Dist. 1	Dist. 2	Dist. 3	Dist. 4	Dist. 5	Dist. 1	Dist. 2	Dist. 3	Dist. 4	Dist. 5	Dist. 1	Dist. 2	Dist. 3	Dist. 4	Dist. 5
Teacher:																				
1. Competence							.32			-.33				-.30						
2. Expectations of Self							.24													
3. Risk Taking																				
4. Interpersonal Orientation							.30				-.41	.34					.31			
5. Attribution Success/Failure																				
6. Orientation to Change					.42										.30					
7. Experiment in Class																				
8. Openness to criticism																				
9. Technical Knowledge							.27					.32								
10. Subject Knowledge																				
11. Experience (Grade)																				
12. Experience (Content)							.33			-.42		.33			-.43					-.38
13. Experience (Teachers Evaluation)	.41		.44		.61		.31	.26		.52		.39	.33		.55		.41	.35		.47
Evaluator:																				
14. Credibility		.62	.66	.58	.74			.36		.31			.40		.46			.43		.38
15. Relationship to Teacher		.60	.53	.56	.57			.31		.30			.34		.44			.31		.44
16. Trustworthiness		.46	.59	.51	.63			.36	.27				.33		.39			.36		.32
17. Interpersonal Manner	.52	.51	.33	.43	.48		.28	.26					.21		.26		.27	.20		.35
18. Patience	.51	.34	.40	.25	.32		.27	.30					.28		.26			.25		.35

153

Appendix C (Cont.)

Largest Correlations Between Items and Criteria by District

	Overall Quality					Attitude					Behavior					Understanding				
	Dist. 1	Dist. 2	Dist. 3	Dist. 4	Dist. 5	Dist. 1	Dist. 2	Dist. 3	Dist. 4	Dist. 5	Dist. 1	Dist. 2	Dist. 3	Dist. 4	Dist. 5	Dist. 1	Dist. 2	Dist. 3	Dist. 4	Dist. 5
19. Flexibility	.36	.49	.38	.51	.50			.24	.34				.17					.21		
20. Technical Knowledge	.60	.55	.50	.43	.61			.31					.40		.31			.40		.29
21. Capacity to Model	.71	.51	.52	.44	.62			.26	.36				.33		.39			.36		.35
22. Familiar with Classroom	.50	.48	.48	.34	.70		.35	.34					.37		.44		.32	.38		.38
23. Experience in Classroom	.40	.47	.49	.39	.69		.32	.29		.34			.33		.49		.33	.36		.41
24. Useful Suggestions	.47	.69	.57	.42	.61		.38	.37	.30	.35			.46	.26	.52		.42	.51		.51
25. Persuasive Rationale	.48	.68	.61	.37	.46		.39	.34	.32			.25	.39	.32	.34		.42	.41	.31	.32
Procedures:																				
26. Standards Communicated		.58	.36	.25	.60					.37					.51		.30	.19		.47
27. Standards Clear		.52	.40	.41	.61													.22		
28. Standards Endorsed	.47	.49	.40	.36	.33		.35	.26					.21				.33	.21		
29. Form of Standards					.35															
30. Standards Unique							.25													
31. Classroom Observation			.32		.47			.25		.36			.24		.36			.27		.44
32. Examine Records			.28		.45			.18	.29	.31			.25		.46			.27		.43
33. Examine Achievement		.45	.29	.37	.32			.18	.28				.27		.28			.23		.34
34. No. of Formal Observations			.22	.25																
35. No. of Informal Observations			.29										.19					.19		
36. Formal Length					.49															

Appendix C (Cont.)

Largest Correlations Between Items and Criteria by District

	Overall Quality					Attitude					Behavior					Understanding				
	Dist. 1	Dist. 2	Dist. 3	Dist. 4	Dist. 5	Dist. 1	Dist. 2	Dist. 3	Dist. 4	Dist. 5	Dist. 1	Dist. 2	Dist. 3	Dist. 4	Dist. 5	Dist. 1	Dist. 2	Dist. 3	Dist. 4	Dist. 5
37. Informal Length									.26				.23					.21		
38. No. of Observers																				
Feedback:																				
39. Amount of Information		.49	.47	.49	.53			.30					.30		.35		.25	.36		
40. Frequency Formal			.37	.51	.52			.32		.37			.29		.48		.26	.34		.44
41. Frequency Informal	.39		.32	.34	.42		.31						.22		.43		.35	.25		.38
42. Depth of Information	.46		.55	.54	.61			.32		.41			.35		.53			.40		.53
43. Quality of Ideas	.72		.58	.54	.46	.42	.36	.32	.29	.31	.43		.35		.44		.31	.44		.42
44. Specificity of Information		.56	.54	.42	.37			.27					.31		.46			.36		.37
45. Nature of Information		.25	.45	.39	.37			.25					.19					.24		
46. Timing of Feedback	.46	.28	.43	.43	.39			.24					.20					.19		
47. Focused on Standards		.44	.45		.31			.22					.20					.27		
Context:																				
48. Time Spent on Evaluation		.28	.41		.49			.21		.36			.21		.53			.21		.47
49. Time for Professional Development	.41		.18	.28	.31		.26			.36			.19		.38		.28	.29		.33
50. Training Available			.18	.27		.46														
51. Clear Evaluation Policy		.41	.36	.36	.56		.26	.20	.29	.40			.24	.28	.48		.36	.17		.43
52. Intended Role		.38	.40	.36	.45		.26	.19	.40			.31	.24	.34	.34		.36	.29		.39
53. Labor Relations		.25	.24		.38		.25	.24					.21					.20		
54. Bargaining Impact									.30					.39						
55. State Law Impact			.24							.31		.39					.37			

References

Beckham, J. C. (1981). *Legal aspects of teacher evaluation.* Topeka, KS: National Organization on Legal Problems in Education.

Bolton, D. L. (1983). *Realistic methods of evaluating competent teachers.* Olympia, WA: School Information and Research Service.

Bolton, D. L. (1973). *Selection and evaluation of teachers.* Berkeley, CA: McCutchan.

Borich, G. D., & Fenton, K. S. (1977). *The appraisal of teaching: Concepts and processes.* Reading, MA: Addison-Wesley.

Bridges, E. M. (1986). *The Incompetent Teacher.* Philadelphia: The Falmer Press.

Connecticut State Department of Education (1979). *Connecticut's teacher evaluation law.* Hartford: Author.

Darling-Hammond, L., Wise, A. E., & Pease, S. R. (1983). *Teacher evaluation in the organizational context: A review of the literature. Review of Educational Research,* 53 (3) 285–327.

Dornbusch, S. M., Deal, T. E., Plumley, D., & Roper,S. S. (1976). *The Collegial Evaluation Program.* Stanford, CA: School of Education, Stanford University.

Dornbusch, S. M., & Scott, W. R. (1975). *Evaluation and the exercise of authority.* San Francisco: Jossey-Bass.

Duke, D. L. (1985). What is the nature of educational excellence and should we try to measure it? *Phi Delta Kappan, 66,* 671–674.

Educational Research Service (1978). *Evaluating teacher performance.* Arlington, VA: Author.

Haertel, E. (1986). The valid use of student performance measures for teacher evaluation. *Educational Evaluation and Policy Analysis, 8*(1), 45–60.

Holley, F. (1982). Personnel education: Essential for success. *CEDR Quarterly. 15*(4). 6–8.

Knapp, M. S. (1982). *Toward the study of teacher evaluation as an organizational process: A review of current research and practice.* Menlo Park, CA: SRI International.

Levin, B. (1979). Teacher evaluation—a review of research. *Educational Leadership. 37*(3). 240–245.

Lewis, A. C. (1982). *Evaluating educational personnel.* Arlington, VA: American Association of School Administrators.

Manatt, R. (1982). *Teacher performance evaluation—Practical application of research.* Occasional Paper 82–1. Ames, IA: Iowa State University.

McGreal, T. L. (1986). Developing a teacher evaluation system: Commonalities of those systems that function effectively. Unpublished paper. University of Illinois, Champaign.

McLaughlin, M. W. (1982). *A preliminary investigation of teacher evaluation practices.* Santa Monica, CA: The Rand Corporation.

McLaughlin, M. W., & Pfeifer, R. S. (1986). Teacher evaluation: Learning for improvement and accountability. Stanford, CA: Stanford Education Policy Institute. Report 86-SEPI-5.

Mitchell, D. E., & Kerchner, C. T. (1983). Labor relations and teacher policy. In L. S. Shulman & G. Sykes (Eds.), *Handbook of teaching and policy.* New York: Longman.

Myers, Donald F. (1973). *Teacher Power.* Lexington, MA: Lexington Books.

National Education Association (1985). *School Personnel Education Manual,* Washington, D.C.: Author.

Natriello, G., & Dornbusch, S. M. (1980–81). *Pitfalls in the evaluation of teachers by principals.* Chicago: University of Chicago.

Natriello, G., & Wilson, B. (1986). Teacher evaluation as an organizational process. A paper presented at the Annual Meeting of the American Educational Research Association, San Francisco, CA.

O'Hanlon, J., & Mortensen, L. (1977). Approaches to teacher evaluation. *CEDR Quarterly. 10*(4). 3–7.

Popham, W. J. (1986). Teacher evaluations: Mission impossible. *Principal. 65*(4). 56–58.

Roper, S. S., & Hoffman, D. E. (1986). *Collegial support for professional improvement.* Eugene, OR: ERIC Clearinghouse in Educational Management Bulletin. *29*(7).

Stark, J. S., & Lowther, M. A. (1984). Predictors of teachers' preferences concerning their evaluations. *Educational Administration Quarterly. 20*(4). 76–106.

Stiggins, R. J. (1986). Teacher evaluation: Accountability and growth—different purposes. *NAASP Bulletin. 70*(490), 51–58.

Stiggins, R. J., & Bridgeford, N. J. (1985). Performance assessment for teacher development. *Educational Evaluation and Policy Analysis. 7*(1), 85–97.

Strike, K., & Bull, B. (1981). Fairness and the legal context of teacher evaluation. In J. Millman (Ed.). *Handbook of teacher evaluation.* Beverly Hills, CA: Sage Publications.

Weick, K. E. (1982). Administering education in loosely coupled schools. *Phi Delta Kappan. 63.* 673–676.

Wise, A. E., Darling-Hammon, L., McLaughlin, M. W., & Bernstein, J. T. (1984). *Teacher evaluation: A study of effective practices.* Santa Monica, CA: The Rand Corporation.

Wood, C. J., & Pohland, P. A. (1979). *Teacher evaluation: Organizational maintenance versus stimulation of improved teaching performance.* Department of Educational Administration, College of Education, University of New Mexico. Las Cruces.

Wuhs, S. K., & Manatt, R. P. (1983). The pace of mandated teacher evaluation picks up. *The American School Board Journal. 170*(4), 28.

Index

teacher involvement in evaluation, 23
teachers working together to promote growth, 37, 67, 71
teaching behaviors, 52
test scores, 75, 126; see also student achievement data
time for evaluation, 22, 23, 36, 91-92
track record of success, 28, 85-86
training for evaluators, 17, 20, 22, 24, 124, 136-137, 141

trust, role of in evaluation for growth, 5, 20, 22, 53, 60, 85, 122

videotaping teacher performance, 17
vision of effective instruction, 74

Weick, 8
Wilson, 122, 125-126, 135
Wise, 1, 8, 121, 125
Wood, 5